49
and holding

49
and holding
RICHARD KNOX SMITH

Introducing Rev. J. Calvin Middy
by Sherman Goodrich

The Two Continents Publishing Group • *Morgan Press*

Library of Congress Cataloging in Publication Data

Smith, Richard Knox.
  49 and holding.

  Bibliography: p.
  1. Middle age. I. Title.
HQ1061.S64   301.43′4   75-11179
ISBN 0-8467-0070-0

Library of Congress Catalog Card Number 75-11179
ISBN 0-8467-0070-0

Production by Planned Production
Text Design by Carol Basen

Printed in U.S.A.

The Two Continents Publishing Group, Ltd
30 East 42 Street
New York 10017
and
Morgan Press

"Lines to an Unhandy Man" Copyright © 1968 by Lois Wyse from the book entitled *Love Poems for the Very Married.* Published by World Publishing and distributed by T. Y. Crowell Company.

"Who Am I?" reprinted with permission of Macmillan Publishing Co., Inc. from *The Cost of Discipleship* (Second Edition) by Dietrich Bonhoeffer. © SCM Press, Ltd. 1959.

"Those Who Have Gone The Route Before" by Richard N. Bolles. Reprinted with permission of Ten Speed Press, Box 4310, Berkeley, CA., from the book *What Color Is Your Parachute?* by Richard N. Bolles.

"The Song of the Widow" reprinted from *Translations from the Poetry of Rainer Maria Rilke* by M.D. Herter Norton. By permission of W. W. Norton & Company, Inc. Copyright © 1938 by W. W. & Company, Inc. Copyright renewed 1966 by M.D. Herter Norton.

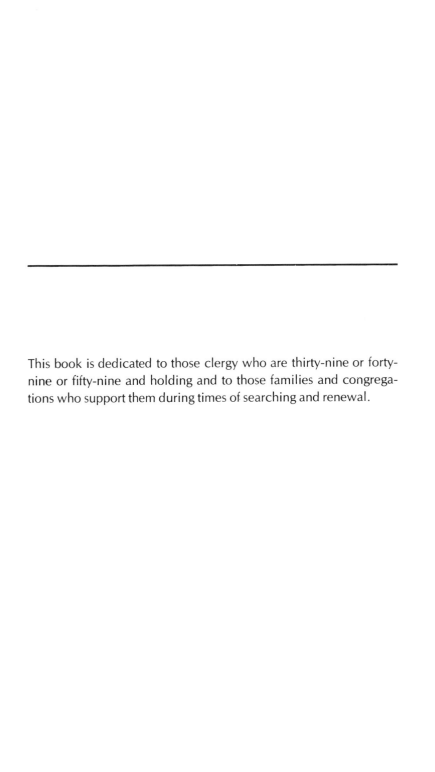

This book is dedicated to those clergy who are thirty-nine or forty-nine or fifty-nine and holding and to those families and congregations who support them during times of searching and renewal.

Reverend Middy? . . . This is the operator! Are you still holding? Reverend Middy? . . .

Contents

Acknowledgements

Books don't get written by one author. They are the products of proddings and patience of a whole cadre of family and friends.

I want to acknowledge my indebtedness at least to the following:

My wife, Harriet, who held me when I was forty-nine and holding.

Dave Poling, who was a mentor to me in this whole project.

Sherman Goodrich, who created Rev. J. Calvin Middy for this book and whose cartoons help us to laugh at ourselves.

Dr. James Callison and L.T. Wade, for reading the manuscript and making technical medical and legal corrections.

Roland Tapp who urged me to finish the manuscript.

Grace Vold who typed the "work" *and Hazel Vance* who did many extra tasks that enabled me to finish.

Introduction

This book was born on the eve of my fiftieth birthday. The time and place of conception are more difficult to date.

Out of my own musings and conversations with contemporaries, I was aware of a "dis-ease" which haunts the clergy at the mid-point of their careers. The symptoms are more than a balding bean and a protruding pot. They are, rather, a restiveness and a personal questioning centering around one's vocational choice. This middle-age malaise is, of course, not confined to the clergy. Psychologists have identified it in a variety of forms. This little book is designed to assist ministers to diagnose their own case and prescribe their own remedy. It is more than an admonition, "Physician, cure yourself," for one of my purposes will be to indicate where help might be available.

While symptoms of the malady may appear the same, the causes and remedies may be quite different with each individual. Therefore, each reader must pick and choose according to his or her own need.

Forty-nine is no magical number. Signs of distress may appear in the early thirties and remain well beyond the half-century mark. One can quickly identify most cases. It is most obvious when a minister remarks, "No church wants to call a pastor who is over fifty."

But forty-nine and holding is the disease of the minister in middle-age who is struggling to know how to make use of the balance of his career.

This certainly is not to imply that there are not many persons who pass through "middlescence" without questions. They need read no further. It is not to overlook the fact that many of the crippling effects of this "dis-ease" are negated when a person has a chance to relocate to a new opportunity and fresh challenge. For those who have found this solution, "cheers and God go with ye."

But if my experience is typical, there are many more who are forty-nine and holding. If you are one of them, this book is for you.

49 and holding

There are many positive things to say about being middle-aged. By the time a person has reached forty-nine, one knows a great deal about oneself. Experience has tested and sharpened skills. Productivity peaks during this period. Maturity enables an evaluation of one's strengths and a friendly family or an understanding cohort point out one's weaknesses. A practiced set of values guides decisions. Well-established routines handle most of the day's activities giving a sense of stability and security.

But the line is narrow between security and boredom. Self-knowledge and satisfaction are not equals. Having skills does not guarantee motivation to use them. Mature reflection has a way of challenging values.

So, if life begins at forty, there are a lot of other things which begin to emerge about the same time. For many ministers, the forties bring an internal struggle between job satisfaction and job frustration. Expectations turn to exasperation just about as often as to excitement. There is a *disillusionment* which comes from discovering that there are many motives besides commitment which guide a congregation in its decisions. There is a *sense of futility* which comes from being consumed in a round of activities, many of which seem meaningless but which dominate the

I've sown, Gladys . . . and I've reaped! Now what?

week's calendar. There is a *despair* at being forty-nine or forty-three or fifty-eight and not being "wanted" by a congregation. There is a *restiveness* which haunts reflective moments producing "middlescent" Walter Mittys. All of this "dis-ease" is here labeled "forty-nine and holding."

Before defining the causes, let's establish the fact that this malaise is curable. The cure begins with acceptance. Acceptance of oneself. Acceptance of the facts of life in all of its dimensions.

And the bulk of this book will give itself to remedies. But H. F. Ellis points out, "Nobody can be helped who is unable to recognize it or is unwilling to own up to it. Admission, as with alcoholics, is an essential preliminary to treatment." But more of cures in another chapter.

I'm home!

THE CRISIS

There is no common definition of "middle-age." One dictionary says it is "the period of human life between youth and old age sometimes considered as the years between forty-five and sixty-five." Barbara Fried, in *The Middle Age Crisis*, puts the lower limits between thirty-eight and forty-five. There are some who push it down even lower into the thirties. It obviously doesn't hit everyone at exactly the same age chronologically. Some contend that the age of one's family or vocation are factors which affect its onset. I have chosen forty-nine because, in the clergy, there is a common feeling that "no church wants to call a minister who is over fifty." Besides, I was forty-nine when I started this book.

Even though there is no unanimity on age, there is wide acceptance of the use of the term "crisis." Those who have the symptoms would agree with this label. The symptoms also have a
commonality among writers in the field. There is a standard use
of such words as: depression, emotional instability, irritability,
anger, despair, anxiety, sexual problems, lack of confidence, and
organic or psychosomatic illness (Barrett). One writer added "an
insidious desire to destroy a way of life which took years to
achieve—to move to another town, to change jobs and spouses."
(Life)

A recent conference called by the American Medical Association composed of experts from varied fields—business, labor,
education, anthropology, medicine—carried the message that this
is the prime of life. However, the purpose of the conference was
to discuss the *problems* of this age group. These were described
as lack of identity, emotional instability, alcoholism, drug abuse,
obesity and lack of physical fitness (Barrett).

"Middle-age," then, seems to be a life crisis rather than an age
span.

Our purpose here is not to present a definitive study on middle-
age but to assist one in identifying with the crisis, to relate some
of the problems of the ministry to it, and to suggest some ways to
deal creatively with it in one's own life.

CAUSES

Like the common cold, there can be both internal and external
factors which produce what Robert Lee has called "Middlescent
malaise." The external causes are those related to our culture and
the way it impinges upon how one feels about oneself. Recogniz-
ing some of the causes should help the minister know that this is
not an occupational malady. Here are some of the causes:

1. Crossing the Generation Gap.

The first cause of the forty-nine syndrome is the idea of aging
itself. We don't like it.

Our society glorifies youthfulness. Vitality, virility and vigour are virtues. Mass media continually remind the peptic generation that the "Pepsi generation" is where it's at! Fortunes are made in hawking aids to make people look younger and hopefully feel younger. All because we have this thing about aging. It might be noted that this reluctance to accept middle-age is not new. Lord Byron contemptuously called middle-age:

> *. . . grim Dante's "obscure wood,"*
> *That horrid equinox, that hateful section*
> *Of human years, that half-way house, that rude*
> *Hut, whence wise travellers drive with circumspection*
> *Life's sad post-horse o'er the dreary frontier*
> *Of Age, and looking back to youth, give one tear.*

Most middle-aged ministers don't actually "give one tear" but they do give a lot of thought. They, too, share the reluctance to give up the youthful image. They, too, want to "live." The result can be anger. One man exploded, "I've grown damned sick and tired of having the youth culture, whatever that is, rammed down my throat." Or the result can just as well be a fearful brooding.

> An anxious fear that time is running out, a vague sense of mental or moral ill-being, a churning sense of self-doubt and disbelief, a general uneasiness at being in the afternoon of life . . . (Lee)

2. Getting Used to Bifocals.

But aging is not just an idea. There are physical effects which, in and of themselves, focus on the changes which are taking place. Cambell Moses, M.D., medical director of the American Heart Association, describes it as a loss of "reserve capacity." "Throughout life," he says, "there are subtle losses in all our body systems, including the central nervous system. By the time a man is 40, he can't escape noticing them." (Schanche)

It does make you look youngish, dear . . . in an oldish sort of way!

Some of the changes he notes: one must work harder to get one's breath; sexual capacity is just not what it used to be; weakening of the eye muscles necessitates bifocals; hearing is not quite as sharp. On the part of some there is a tendency during this period to be convinced one is really sick and to brood over both real and imagined degeneration of one's physical condition. Every time one puts on a swimming suit or tries to read with the bifocals is a reminder that "he ain't what he used to be."

3. There Is No Place to Hide.

The third cause of the forty-niner hesitation is crisis fatigue. The pace of life is more than one can take. Dr. Saxes writes, "The American man of forty to sixty is, almost literally the man in the middle, caught up in a world of pressures . . . He is badgered, bamboozled and bedeviled." (Saxes) *Changing Times'* Dr. Bigelow Wynkoof (to rhyme with win spoof) put it in layman's terminology, "The people are pooped." (*Changing Times*)

It is not just the pace of the individual. Constant confrontation by the problems of society and the absence of anything which guarantees stability takes its toll. Events no longer creep in on "petty pace." They hammer relentlessly from all angles beating down the will and pulverizing the spirit. Allan Toffler's book *Future Shock* topped the best seller list because he described how people felt. Anyone who takes the world seriously can identify with the author of "Stop the World, I Want to Get Off."

4. But I Am the Boss.

What does a person do to make one's work challenging after twenty-five years? According to the Peter Principle, one should have reached the "level of incompetence" by this time. More generously, it means having arrived at about the level of success in one's field. Some jobs are regarded as a means of livelihood and have been a bore from the beginning. But most of the professions have been chosen as an adventure. They become routine.

Peter Drucker identifies what he calls "knowledge workers." These are people who manage knowledge, the essential of our modern society. Drucker feels that this group is especially vulnerable to a middle-age career crisis. Ministers fit into this category as would lawyers, doctors, engineers, middle management personnel, university professors, military officers and others. He writes:

There's times, Gladys, when I feel I'd like to run away and join
a circus! That's when I realize I already have!

The accomplished knowledge journeyman, at forty-five or
fifty, is in his physical and mental prime. If he is tired and
bored, it is because he has reached the limit of contribution
and growth in his first career—and he knows it. He is likely
to deteriorate rapidly if left to doing what no longer truly
challenges him. It is of little use to look to "hobbies" or to
"cultural interests" to keep him alive. Being an amateur
does not satisfy a man who has learned to be a professional.
He may be willing, as he gets older, to spend a little more
time on "interests" outside his job. But he is not willing,
nor emotionally able, to make such "interests" the center
of his life, even if he has the money to do so. To be a
dilettante has to be learned in childhood as all aristocracies
have known. (Drucker)

One respondent in a study under the auspices of Yale University indicated that he had often dreamed of fame and success. He described his mid-life disappointments this way: "I feel a weakening of the need to be a great man and an increasing feeling of let's just get through this the best way we can. Never mind hitting any home runs. Let's just get through the ball game without getting beaned." (Scarf)

This attitude often prompts persons to look for other "more exciting" types of employment. A director of an executive placement service indicated that most of those who come to him *think* there are fewer thorns on the other side of the arroyo. Other professions are idealized to have less problems, tensions and frustrations than the current one.

In short, if there is no up, a man gets restless. If he was motivated by success (or power or wealth), he realizes that opportunities for advancement are decreasing. For the minister, the mails no longer bring offers from other parishes. For the professional, there is little spark to grow or develop.

5. What Did You Do for Me Recently.

There are also peer expectations, real or imagined, which prevent a person from being at ease. There are pressures, overt or implied, from family and friends which contribute to a person's dissatisfaction with present status. Success is not a noun or a goal. It is an insatiable verb. Being "other directed" has pushed people to demand of themselves achievements which they might have been content to have passed to others. In the ministry, it is the unwillingness to move laterally or to a smaller church because it implies failure in the eyes of others.

Maria Levinson, one of the psychologists in a study conducted at Yale University, says that in some cases "it was the wife, not the husband who upset the equilibrium, who demands for him to get out of his rut and start changing." (Scarf)

Even if one is satisfied to settle in, this is not always possible. There will be those who, in their rush to the top of the "caterpillar pillar" will push and claw from below in their scramble to

How can you sit there and ask me what I *really* want out of
life? Look at me, man. . . . I'm a bishop!

get ahead. There are jobs and churches who become impatient
with an incumbent who becomes incompetent.

6. Was It Worth It?

Perhaps the most difficult cause to analyze is the questioning of
one's values which often floats just under the surface of other
symptoms. Now that I've come this far, was it worth it? What is
life all about anyway? Who am I? Iver Brooks was a successful
stockbroker until he began to question his life. "When I asked
myself if this is really what I want to do for the next five or ten
years, the answer was, no." (*Life*)

These questions may emerge in discussion with sons or daughters who have a way of challenging the values of parents. It may
come because the salary increase or new boat did not bring the

Well, as soon as you *do* discover the meaning of it all, come in and wash up for supper!

sense of fulfillment savored in its contemplation. It may result as a lingering thought which came to mind at the funeral of a friend or parent. Reflection is a characteristic of middle-age and any ripple on the surface of quietude disturbs reflections.

Beyond these "external causes," a minister finds some vocational pressures which intensify his own ennui. (Don't look it up, it means feeling of uneasiness or discontent.)

1. No Mail Today (Or Many Are Called But Few Are Chosen)

Not only is it difficult to move to "fields of larger service," it is just plain difficult to move. If the "availability of full-time salaried jobs" is a criteria, there is no shortage of trained clergy. A study in the United Presbyterian Church indicated a marked trend toward more ministers within the denomination at a time when there is a decreasing number of churches. One doesn't need to be a prophet to see how this complicates the possibilities of relocation.

The Rev. Richard Bolles is so convinced that some men will be *unable* to locate within the church that he has written a knowledgeable guide for seeking a second career outside of the church. It is called *What Color Is Your Parachute?*

My own personal observation is that the most enervating experience in a pastor's life is to want to move and to be unable to do so. His desire may be personally evoked or congregationally provoked but the frustrations are the same.

There has been much written in the past few years about the number of people leaving the ministry. No doubt some of this can be traced to a "faith crisis." However, the authors of *Ex-Pastors*, a study of men who have left the ministry, report to the contrary. "Our findings give no encouragement to the view that loss of faith is responsible for moves into secular work." (Jud) Their conclusions confirm my impressions that "men were pushed rather than pulled out of church employment." This lack of opportunity is demoralizing.

2. Boxed-In

A second cause is closely related to the difficulty in receiving a call to another church. It is the "boxed-in" feeling that comes from not having any other alternative. One would think that four years of college and three years of graduate school ought to make one good for something. It seems, however, only to make one good for goodness' sake. Professional training for the clergy does not provide any other direct marketable skill. True, there are some closely related to such fields as teaching, counseling and administration, but most require advanced degrees or training. At "forty-nine and holding" one is faced with college bills for offspring, a value held high by members of the manse. It is no time for Dad to become Joe College.

If the meek *do* inherit the earth, there'll be a lien against it within six months!

3. Funny, You Don't Look Like a Clergyman

Role conflict is the third cause of "dis-ease." A recent book, *Clergy In The Cross-Fire*, (Smith) explores the dimensions of unrest in the lives of ministers due to "the contradictions between the kind of person he knows himself to be and the demands that his job makes upon him." This, of course, is not confined to age but it is never-the-less a factor among those of mid-career.

Dear Lord, please help me to have patience. And hurry!

Idealism surrounds the "call" to the ministry. Both the church and those called have their own images of what a pastor ought to be and do. The expectations are not always shared. Recent changes in the life of the church have decreased the possibility that they are even compatible. Every minister can recount the events surrounding the demise of a friend or classmate. Each repeat undermines his own sense of confidence.

A closely related experience plagues the quiet hours of many a person of the cloth. His job is not what he expected. He is disillusioned with his own life. When one has made a covenant with God, all vocational questions become faith crises. What you see is not always what you get. More than one member of the clergy will nod in agreement to the words of Henri Nouwen:

> The painful irony is that the minister, who wants to touch the center of men's lives, finds himself on the periphera,

often pleading in vain for admission. He never seems to be where the action is, where the plans are made and the strategies discussed. He always seems to arrive at the wrong place at the wrong time with the wrong people, outside the walls of the city when the feast is over, with a few crying women. (Nouwen)

These are some of the causes which tend to hold back the minister from enthusiastically saying, "Fifty is fine."

Saying Yes to Life

T here are times in life when significant questions demand significant answers. Middle-age is one such time. The romance of choosing a mate or the adventure of a first job may be missing but the decisions pulse with possibilities. Resolving what one will do with the fifteen years of productivity should not be treated casually. Enriching what should be one-third of a life-time is not unimportant. Providing half of the memories for a golden wedding anniversary celebration is worthy of attention. Tempered by increasing self-understanding and mellowed by experience, these mid-career musings sparkle with potential.

Erik Erikson has written of the middle years, ". . . . in this stage a man and a woman must have defined for themselves what and whom they have come to care for, what they care to do well, and how they plan to care for what they have started and created." (Erikson)

One more should be added: By the time a person is in the middle years, he or she should know *who they are*, who and what is important to them, what they can do best, and what they want to spend their time doing.

This is easy to say. Part of the "dis-ease" of middle-age is the haunting feeling that one should know the answers to these very queries and does not.

The identity crisis of "middlescence" has not received as extensive study as adolesence but it is just as real to those involved. There is confusion as to who we are. We have some vague feelings about what we do well and there is ambivalence about what we want to do with the rest of our lives. That's the rub!

THE FRINGE BENEFITS

But these frustrations also hold some hope for our relief. They are prods to our thinking and evaluation. If we are forty-nine and holding, there is only one alternative to becoming fifty. We might start by thinking about that!

We might also recognize that the weariness and anxieties which face ministers are not unlike those which plague a large portion of the congregation on any given Sunday morning. For in that congregation there will be those who have deep questions about their health, jobs, future and about themselves. To ponder who we are and what our faith says to us is, indeed, part of our identification with those we would serve even as it is part of our self-identification.

Howard Thurman has written, "It is good to pause to make an end of so much that bothers and harrasses the spirit, to assess the meaning of our lives in the light of the movement of the Spirit within us." (Thurman) By the act of assessment and appraisal, we begin to clarify our purposes and reaffirm the basic commitments of our lives.

IF YOU CAN'T LICK 'EM

But as pages in the datebook go by one-by-one—used or unused, we can become Macbethian in our fatalism. The tomorrows not only creep in on a "petty pace from day to day," they all look alike. It takes no great effort or imagination to become passive to this parade. No extensive search is required in our circle of friendships to identify a long list of those who choose the "whats-the-use" syndrome. They are characterized by pessimism, lack of personal care, disinterest in causes or issues, and a general "play it safe" approach to making decisions. In short it is called "resignation."

There may be secondary signs of irritability, low personal expectations and highly critical verbalization of expectations of one's children or spouse.

But at forty-nine, it ought to be possible to recognize the difference between resignation and acceptance.

Resignation is the passive adaptation to events and situations over which one seems to have no control.

Acceptance, on the other hand, can be a creative response seeking alternative possibilities of relating to the same events and situations. Erik Erikson defines these two "developmental manifestations" at this stage in life as "stagnation" and "generativity." Much of life for the self-actualized person is response. Obviously, the results will be different if the response is active or passive, acceptance or resignation, stagnation or generativity.

I've resigned myself to the fact that I resign myself to too many facts!

Tournier emphasizes the necessity of saying "yes" to life. "There arises a malaise, the moment there is disharmony between me and myself, between what I affect to be and what I am ... there is a profound joy as soon as I make a readjustment of me to fit my reality. . . . The most difficult and unhappiest people are those who cannot accept the world and life as they are, with sickness, old age, and death; those who cannot learn abandonment, who cannot bear to be contradicted, who have nothing but complaints, and criticism, who cannot accept themselves, with their limitations, their infirmity and their dependence." (Tournier)

The problem is that this creeps up on us at middle-age. All of a sudden we realize that it is there. A widow in one of Maria Rilke's poems senses this:

> *Life was good to me in the beginning.*
> *It kept me warm, it gave me zest.*
> *That it does so to all the young.*
> *how could I know that then?*
> *I did not know what living was—,*
> *suddenly it was just year on year,*
> *no more good, no more new, no more wonderful,*
> *as if torn in two in the middle.* (RILKE)

Isn't this the tragedy of middle-age, the void in the middle? "No more good, no more new, no more wonderful." Those are expressions of an attitude. Life has not changed all that much.

Resignation or stagnation is a dead-end rut. A road map is not needed to know its destination. Acceptance is open ended. Its direction may be implied but there are choices or routes and some variations possible in the scenery.

SAYING YES TO LIFE

Acceptance is essential to breaking the "holding pattern." Acceptance that aging is a daily fact of life and neither needs to be denied nor feared. Acceptance that emotional changes and physical limitations are part both of growing up and growing old. Acceptance that death is one facet of human existence which can intrude upon our awareness without overpowering or debilitating us.

In his book, *Learn to Grow Old,* which is quoted above and which I would commend to anyone in the "holding pattern," Paul

I've learned to accept life for what it is, bishop! I'm just not positive that it accepts me on the same terms!

Tournier says, "To accept is to say 'yes' to life in its entirety." To affirm life in all of its fullness is to affirm life in the fullness of time. We have no choice to becoming fifty and more but we do have some alternatives as to our attitude and our affirmations about it.

Some of us are crushed by the inevitable. Others ride with it, adapt to it and even adapt it to themselves. Those who are open will be able to cope. Those who deny or resist will be in for trouble. L. P. Saxes writes:

> The basic problem of the man of middle years is his aware- ness of the fact that he is mortal, that he is growing older, that time is beginning to run out.
>
> How he reacts to this knowledge is all important to his future happiness. If he calmly accepts the inevitability of

Love thy neighbor as thyself! Love thy neighbor as thyself!
Love thy neighbor . . .!

old age and death, but realizes he had many fruitful, con-
tented years ahead, he will be happy. If he tries to fight
against the inevitable, he may cause himself great suffering.
(Saxes)

Saying "yes" to life moves us from the passive to the active.
The very saying of the word is affirmation. Even pronouncing it
brings changes to our orientation, establishes our bearings, alerts
us to possibilities, attunes us to a whole new set of what the youth
have called "vibrations."

Saying "yes" to life is not superficial smiles, glib grins or goad-
ed guffaws. It is not dancing in the streets oblivious to the world's

wounds. It's not stoic song or cocktail conversation. The time we are most aware of the realities of ourselves and our society is when we can say "yes" with meaning and conviction.

Dag Hammarskjold sums it up when he wrote, "It is never to be forgotten that the yes to destiny is included in the yes to God. This does not require . . . that we are to see every occurrence as a reflection of the will of God; there are also destructive powers at work in the drama of existence. It means, rather, that in every event of life there is a meaning supplied by God, to be realized by man. In that sense, to say 'yes' to destiny is to say yes to God and to his will—and thus life becomes meaningful and destiny is not a chilly and meaningless fate. Life takes on meaning when destiny is seen as reflecting the will of God and operative in the choice of man."(Aulen)

There are many, some would say most, men and women who go through this period of reappraisal and make of it a time of renewal and growth. We can too.

Here are four areas in which a minister will need to do some accepting: the aging process itself, physical changes, death and self-image.

DARLING, I AM GROWING OLD

The first adjustment is to just accept the fact that all of us, this includes me, are aging. Most of us feel more like spectators to this process than participants in it. How many people have you heard joke about going to a class reunion and laughing about how everyone else has changed!

Middle-age may be a tough term to define but it may not be necessary to try. It can be as elusive as a mood or as vague as a feeling but if we are there, we will know it. Let's accept the fact that we are not as young as we once were and go from there.

Too often, we try to be something other than our plain old middle-aged self. It is a matter of acting our age. No argument can be made against staying alert, vital, creative, venturesome, open, imaginative, unless they are contrasted with aging. Too

You're only as old as you feel, Gladys! I'd still be young if it weren't for that!

much is written on how to stay "young" all your life. We need rather to know now to mature (age) with flexibility and adapt with understanding. Being bored or sloppy or dull or lazy are not age characteristics. Middle-age is a reality not a crime.

In writing about how people are afraid to lose their youth, H. F. Ellis has said, "the lesson must be ceaselessly inculcated that the crown and goal of middle-age is to be as unlike teen-agers as possible." (Ellis) Recognition of who and what we are is half-way to acceptance. This has been our own experience and the claim of the gospel which we have preached. Even so, the realization of our limitations in new areas often comes as a shock. The truth can often hit us just that way.

Adjustment will be needed in our thinking. The realization that we will never accomplish all that we had hoped to do or be all that we had hoped to become can be discouraging. All of life is a task. A task which will never be finished. We must learn to live knowing that we will leave unfinished tasks and uncompleted projects and unfulfilled hopes.

This may also be a reason for reordering one's priorities. I know one minister and his wife who have rearranged their life-style to do some of the things now which were scheduled for the future. They say that too many of their friends postponed plans and trips until later and death or illness meant that they were never done. There is the assumption that we can project our lives into the future as an extension of the present. But aging changes, often abruptly, what that future will be. Acceptance of this fact will give a more valid understanding of the present and how we use it. If something by nature will be left undone, what are the things we want to be sure to have done?

SILVER THREADS AMONG THE GOLD

Physiological changes bug us the most. "Outward and visible manifestations of an inward grace," we hardly treat them as sacraments.

A TV show entitled "The Male Menopause" struck such a responsive chord in our community that it was repeated four times by popular demand. The awareness of change in life at midpoint has long been accepted by women. The changes which affect men may not be as serious or as definable but they do happen. We need to adjust to them.

—— If the forehead has been creeping to include the whole head, don't panic. Bald headed men get lovin' too.
—— Does it take a little longer to get moving in the morning? That's okay. With your experience you won't need as much time to do that job.
—— Do you now take a 36 waist on your pants? You'd better work on that!
—— Have you grey around the temples? It makes you look very distinguished.

As much as we stereotype ministers, they are not all clergy-*men.* A woman can best describe these physiological changes from a female perspective.

In the middle-aged struggle for selfhood, it is not an easy matter to find ourselves faced with not only our internal

Good Lord . . . another character line!

conflicts about our sex roles, but also embroiled in the midst
of a social revolution concerned with this issue. There we
are, trying to face what menopause, or the empty nest or
retirement will mean to our sense of ourselves as women,
and we are caught in the midst of a battle about what it
means to be a woman from birth to death! For those of us

who have been turning inward to try to discover our own feelings, it sometimes seems almost more than we can bear to be constantly reminded of the larger issues. Especially since we are inclined to feel that what ever happens in the current upheaval will be too late to influence our lives. (LeShan)

But here again not all is doomsville.

— Have you gone to bifocals? Dorothy Parker was wrong. Men still make passes at girls who wear glasses.
— Are you putting on weight in odd places? No excuse for that!
— Have brown curls begun to show silver? Some of the most charming people in the world have grey hair.
— Are you worried about those wrinkles? They seem to make your eyes sparkle.

There are some rewards which come with the aging process. One is deference. The younger generation will make some allowances which we ought to accept with grace and relief. Dr. Ellis has said,

Giving things up is or should be one of the great consolations of middle-age. The man of fifty-plus, waving 'goodby' from his desk-chair with a resigned 'off you go and enjoy yourselves. I'm too old for that kind of thing now,' is a living proof of the essential beneficience of the natural processes. There is a strong sense of release. The annoyance of not being able to do some things as well as he used to can be terminated, the wise man of forty-five suddenly realizes, by not doing it. The pity is he did not realize it at forty. (Ellis)

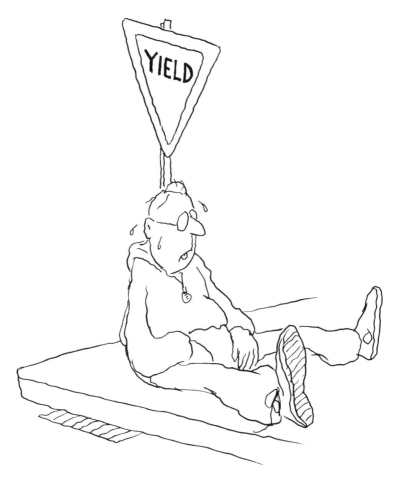

Now, I'm not going to be embarrassed when my sons laugh at the way my knees look when I water ski. In fact, I don't think that I will water ski!

This is not to say that there aren't serious adjustments which can come at this time. Diabetes, breast cancer, hearing decline, heart conditions all strike during this period. Radical reorganization of habits may be necessary. But this is where maturity benefits. Learning to pace oneself, to use energy wisely, to draw out of the resources of experience. This is the seasoning of life. Eda LeShan writes, ''The essence of whether one experiences a "renaissance" or the 'Dark Ages' in middle life seems to me to depend a great deal on the degree to which one can use change effectively, rather than denying its existence and trying to get on with business as usual.'' (LeShan)

LIFE IS FADING FAST AWAY

That line from the old song sounds a bit heavy doesn't it? What has the middle-age malaise to do with one's attitude toward death? Ultimately, both are tied up with our understanding of the nature, meaning and purpose of life itself. During the middle years, there is a growing awareness of death, which is consciously or unconsciously pushing in on our thinking and perspectives.

Dr. Kenn Rogers of Cleveland State University is convinced that there are two observable modes of behavior during the midlife crisis, ''flight from or fight with one's fear of death.'' (Rogers) This may be too strong for the clergy, for haven't we been in frequent contact with death? But even for the pastor who has often stood by the open grave, the fact of one's own death may be far removed. In fact, the very handling of the hurts and heartaches of parishioners may require that a minister build a protective shell which isolates thoughts of death from family or self. I recently heard one minister remark, ''That was the first time that one of my really close friends died and it shook me up.''

This is also a time when many will experience the death of parents. There is a startling realization at the death of a parent that one can never go back. It is a bench mark in personal experiences. Even in our culture with families spread across the miles and where there is little close contact or communication, the death of a parent has a finality to it which has never quite been known before.

It is perhaps at this point that ministers are basically better equipped to handle the sobering and sometimes depressing feel-

Do you realize that in only twenty six more years I'll be seventy five!!

ings which can be related to this part of the "dis-ease" of the person in the middle. But it can also be a time when reality forces a crisis to a person's own faith. There is a new challenge to the validity of what has been proclaimed from the pulpit so many times, "This is eternal life, that they know thee, the only true God, and Jesus Christ whom you have sent." We find with Brother Lawrence that death is never far behind us and that we should be prepared to face it, "For we die but once, and a miscarriage . . . is irretrievable."

But My Darling You Will Be

It may be quite a shock to discover that others don't see us as the dashing, bright young theologian ready for whatever may come. We must bring our self-image up-to-date as part of the acceptance of change. We always carry around a concept of who we are. Most often it is in terms of what we do. When people introduce themselves in a group, identity is established as teacher, housewife, farmer, lawyer or pastor of St. Elizabeth's Presbyterian Church.

In other contexts, relationships may be stressed. I am Harriet's husband, Kirk and Paul's father or Joe and Mabel's son. Minority consciousness has been developed lately which gives an appreciation of racial identity. As we work through the middle-age crisis, we must tailor these terms and develop other ones to define who we are *now*. Dr. Edward Klein points out that as the father of a young child, there is a whole constellation of images which one has of his authority and place in the family. These change (or should) when the children are grown and married. We may not realize that we are still treating them as "children" but they do and they resent it. They know they have changed; we may not realize that we have, too. (Scarf)

It is often quite a revelation to discover yourself as a person apart from the normal ways in which you are known. One recently retired minister refused to take a preaching assignment in a new community to which he had just moved. "They don't yet know that I'm a minister and I am having such fun just being treated as a person," he explained. "Maybe later. . . ."

All of us have an image of who and what we are. To the extent that we are able to fulfill this image, we are content or thwarted. Dr. Margaretta Bowers says, "The clergy suffer terribly from this need to be what they feel they should be, that they know their congregations expect them to be." Don Smith in *Clergy in the Cross-Fire* documents the kinds of tensions and frustrations which have developed because of the change of role expectations by congregations. When these two dynamics are put together, it is no wonder that there is a "dis-ease" among the clergy at mid-career. One minister wrote, "For a long time I said, 'no' to my own existence. I ran around trying to be someone else other people told me I was or should be. I played a lot of roles to hide myself, my loneliness, my weakness, my fears, and my resentment. But I paid a high emotional price for it in anxiety, depression and pounding headaches." (Sueltz)

Here are some positive things which we can do to help us accept who we are as professionals.

1. We can reaffirm the validity of the ministry as a profession. Even within the clergy, during the last few years, there has been

I finally learned not to fear death, reverend. Now *life* scares the hell out of me!

an apologetic attitude toward the image of ministry. We often hear remarks about the minister as the "paid people lover." Except that there are too many underpaid, there is nothing wrong with being a people lover. There are some who are pretty difficult to love with or without salary, but the very nature of our task and commitment is a love for people. "By this shall men know you are my disciples, that you love one another."

Hey baby . . . you're a minister! Far out! me too!!

2. We can stop measuring our total effectiveness by temporary standards. I was in one group of pastors who were flailing themselves and the church for its racism. They were ready to give an ultimatum to their constituency: "either get with it or get out." There is little question that racism is a key issue of our day and it insidiously corrupts the church. Without minimizing its viciousness or our urgency to face the issue, racism is still only sin. It is one of the obvious sins to condemn at this point in history. But

the church, whether we like it or not, is still composed of sinners and will be, even if all of the racists have been purged. We cannot measure the church's ultimate effectiveness on any temporary standard. There are deeper and more basic human conditions of which we are all a part.

3. We should stop rejecting the church or its people when they don't live up to our criteria. This tension between what we are and what we ought to be is a mark of any Christian life. The church has always made this odd claim that, ridiculous as it might seem, somehow we are God's people. On the one hand is the danger of thinking we are his because we are good or because we do what he wants us to do. On the other hand is the danger of becoming morose or pessimistic because we don't see how, with all of our faults, we could possibly be the church.

We are not God's people because we are obedient. Hopefully, we become obedient when we realize we are his. Our children do not become ours because they do what we tell them. But more and more as they sense the love which surrounds them, they live as members of the family. We are God's pastors, we are his church because he acted and is acting to make us so.

These are questions which will haunt us every day:

—— Without becoming smug or sterile, how do we accept ourselves with all of our pettiness and shortcomings and still live knowing that we have been accepted by him?

—— With all of our faults and prejudices and frailties, how do we accept our constituency as the Body of Christ without creating the impression that we have attained the fullness of his stature?

—— With all of its vested interests and cultural accretions, how do we accept the church and still continue to grow in our understanding of what it means to be his people in this kind of a world?

Don't *any* of you have *any* idea what I'm trying to say?

Don't allow a quarter of a century of seasoned inside knowledge of your own failings or the soft spots in your ministry to blur the mystery and wonder of that call which prompted you to say, "Here am I, Lord."

Dietrich Bonhoeffer captures this awe in his poem called "Who Am I?"

> *Who am I? They often tell me*
> *I would step from my cell's confinement*
> *calmly, cheerfully, firmly,*
> *like a squire from his country house.*
> *Who am I? They often tell me*
> *I would talk to my warders*
> *freely and friendly and clearly,*
> *as though it were mine to command.*
> *Who am I? They also tell me*
> *I would bear the days of misfortune*
> *equably, smilingly, proudly,*
> *like one accustomed to win.*
>
> *Am I then really all that which other men tell of?*
> *Or am I only what I know of myself,*
> *restless and longing and sick, like a bird in a cage,*
> *struggling for breath, as though hands were compress-*
> *   ing my throat*
> *yearning for colours, for flowers, for the voices of*
> *   birds,*
> *thirsting for words of kindness, for neighbourliness,*
> *tossing in expectation of great events,*
> *powerlessly trembling for friends at an infinite*
> *   distance,*
> *weary and empty at praying, at thinking, at making,*
> *faint, and ready to say farewell to it all?*
>
> *Who am I? This or the other?*
> *Am I one person today and tomorrow another?*
> *Am I both at once? A hypocrite before others, and*
> *   before myself a contemptibly woebegone weak-*
> *   ling?*

Or is something within me still like a beaten army,
fleeing in disorder from victory already achieved?
Who am I? They mock me, these lonely questions of
*   mine.*
Whoever I am, thou knowest, O God, I am thine.

Watch Those Side Effects

Since so much of our lives and identity is encompassed in our vocational role, we are apt to be "blind-sided" by problems which seem unrelated. As we concentrate on solving the frustrations of our role as teacher, lawyer, engineer or minister, we may complicate our relationships as husband or father. If our job satisfactions diminish, excitement may be sought in extra-marital affairs. If the morning routine is a bore, maybe a couple of martinis at lunch will shorten the hours until dinner. If it is possible to "get by" with little effort at the office, why bother to keep trim physically or mentally?

Middle-age is a time of high risk to personal habits, and family relationships. The psychological and physical changes bring on what often seems to be irrational actions. A sudden heart attack ends a life of a friend who only last week seemed in the best of health. A man leaves his wife of 20 years and becomes a "swinger." A couple who seemingly were always on the edge of a divorce, find a new zest for their marriage. A personable minister who was popular as a preacher and counselor leaves a suburban parish to become a car salesman. While the actions may seem irrational, there is a frequent enough pattern to alert us to some of the areas of danger.

TENNIS ANYONE

It is no secret that "middlescence" is a time of health hazards. One man said that he now reads the obituaries for people of his own age. Those who die younger he knows are probably accidents but those "my age usually go with a heart attack." That may not be a scientific sampling but it is accurate enough to alert us to some of the danger spots. Here are some helpful hints:

1. Get a medical check-up. This is the time to begin the practice of annual physicals if you are not in the habit. Any unintended weight loss or change in bowel habits should be brought immediately to the attention of a physician. An electrocardiogram will establish a baseline record from which doctors can determine any significant change in the future. Cancer is often discovered in routine check-ups before symptoms appear. Early diagnosis enhances the possibilities of a cure. Elevated cholesterol or sugar in the blood may be controlled by diet if found early enough. A doctor's orders to "watch that weight" or "get that exercise" will do much to steel otherwise weak resolutions to do the Canadian Air Force exercises.

2. Watch your food intake. A friend of mine recently went on a diet. "Every pound you carry over what you weighed when you graduated from high school will take one year off your life," he says. This may not be factual, but it encouraged him to lose 15 pounds. He looks and feels better. One medical group has said that weight-control, exercise and a limit to smoking are "the three keys to longer life."

3. Exercise regularly. Many claim evidence to indicate that it is the greatest single factor in preventing coronary thrombosis. Exercise may be a grind, but the President's Health Council suggests that 11 minutes a day will make a difference. They also urge turning everyday activities into helpful exercise. Here are some of their ideas:

So I told the doctor I sometimes feel tired and lonely . . . and
he recommended jogging!

—— give yourself a vigorous rub-down with a rough towel
after a shower.

—— lift your chair. Don't shove it.

—— welcome an opportunity to walk.

—— climb stairs two at a time.

An excess of 100 calories a day can result in as much as a 10
pound gain in weight over a year's time. These same calories can
be burned off with a daily walk of 15-20 minutes.

4. Learn to unwind. (This section added by the author's wife.)
Take some time off for play. Put your feet on the desk. Try a cat-
nap. Laugh. Did it ever occur to you that in the middle of the
most hectic week of his life (Holy Week), Jesus took a day off?

5. Learn the symptoms of a heart attack. Leon went home from

an office party emotionally drained and tired. In the middle of the night, he was stabbed awake by severe chest pains. He argued himself out of waiting till morning to see if they would go away. Instead, he drove himself to the hospital and was told he was in the middle of a mild heart attack. His prompt action reduced the time of recovery and the extent of damage.

Pains which are warnings of a heart attack may occur in a variety of locations. The most frequent constellation are in the chest and arms, chest and neck, chest and back or upper abdomen. The pain in the chest may be in the center, and is usually felt as a sensation of pressure or squeezing rather than a jabbing sensation. A doctor friend described it as having someone hit you with his fist right in the middle of the chest. The symptoms are dramatic. Breathlessness, nausea, and sweating when connected with pain are ominous. Don't chance it. Get to a doctor.

FOR BETTER OR FOR WORSE

Middle-age is a crisis time for marriage. As long ago as 1965, one fourth of all divorces filed in this country were of those who had been married 15 years or longer. Maggie Scarf reports that the rate of marital break-up during the "twenty-year slump" appears to be increasing every year. The causes for this are very much parallel to those generally applied to those symptoms of middle-age that have been here called a "dis-ease." There is often a growing but almost an imperceptible break-down in communication which becomes apparent when the children leave home and there is no one left with whom to talk. Physical changes need to be accepted both by one's self and in one's spouse. If a couple has been held together for the sake of the children, the glue disappears as the children gain independence. The common interests and satisfactions which brought them together may have given way to new interests. Marriage mystique may dissolve under curlers for breakfast and face cream for bed. Little habits which annoy may grow to be intolerable. Or it may just be plain boredom.

I am unaware of any studies on divorce among the clergy. However, break-up of families is not uncommon. While there are some congregations where it would be anathema, a divorce does not necessitate ending meaningful service to the church. No doubt, a divorced clergyperson would have to make some initial adjustments in employment or location but it is not impossible.

Marriage problems, however, have been the reason for some people to leave the ministry in mid-career. There seems to be a spiral effect. Middle-age "dis-ease" affects the marriage and marriage problems intensify the feelings of inadequacy and lack of fulfillment putting more tension into the marriage relationship. Even under the best circumstances, there are times when we are hard to love and times when it is difficult to love others. When we don't feel good about ourselves we are not apt to feel good toward anyone. Given two stressed middle-age people, the stress will affect not only each other but everything they do.

All of this may be further complicated by an unfulfilled sex life. Robert Lee quotes an old saying, "When sexual adjustment in a marriage is good, it constitutes about 10 per cent of the positive part, but when sexual adjustment is bad, it constitutes about 90 per cent of what is wrong." (Lee)

If at forty-nine, you are suddenly aware that there are problems in your marriage, consult a good marriage counselor. You have probably seen this enough to know the complications which you face and the hurt and heartache which can result.

If you don't sense any problem, good, but it is still important to recognize this is a time for sensitivity. My wife and I are repeatedly thankful to each other and to God for making our relationship one which is growing and personally satisfying and stimulating to each other.

There are some elements which can be introduced into a marriage which can enrich relationships and deepen the values of marriage during this time of "middlescence" and beyond.

What you both need is more exercise, lots of fresh air, a better diet, and a dirty movie once in a while!

1. Adapt your family life patterns to the present and the future and don't try to recreate the past or depend upon the way things (or people) were. My wife must learn to live with a balding, bifocaled, bulging fifty-year-old man. I must accept her, wrinkles, pills and diet. One man who just learned that he was a grandfather, said that he could adjust to that idea but he wasn't sure that he was excited about being married to a grandmother.

2. Look for ways to enrich your sex life. Sexual mores and acceptances have made drastic changes since we were launched. There is readily available from any bookstore or library some excellent material which will add something to your understand-

TODAY'S
SERMON

the
SEX
REVOLUTION
REVISED
AT 8 AM
AND 11 AM

Where was the sex revolution when I was still able to revolt?

ings. It isn't necessary to practice everything suggested. The purpose is to bring joy and satisfaction to the sex act. One Roman Catholic theologian says, "Love making is an act of the human person, of intelligence and sensitivity, of gentleness and respect for one another, of struggle and of happy combat. The whole psyche is involved in it; one's skin, one's emotions, one's juices,

But what if the congregation found out?

one's mind, one's perceptions, one's freedom, one's aspirations. Animals have babies but they do not make love. Human beings create an art of playfulness and make love not when they need to but when they wish.'' (Novak)

The results of a hysterectomy or the use of the pill can well bring a new sense of freedom resulting in an increasingly satisfying sex life for the middle-aged couple.

My wife and I do our own things! I play golf, bowl, fish, and coach little league! *She* cooks!

3. Build in some times for doing one's own thing. With no children around, there may be a tendency to feel that a couple must always do things together. If there is a maturity in relationships and also in our own understanding of the personal growth needs of each other, this can be done as an enriching experience for each as an individual and through sharing a growing number of exciting experiences.

The more that each of us brings to this relationship, the more interesting it will be. One does not need to understand art to have a home beautified by a wife's "being into" painting. It is not necessary to be able to sing to enjoy a husband's love for music.

Of course I enjoy your company! Now please, leave me alone!

A person who has cultivated interests and outlets for interests and skills is a person who is more fun to be with.

4. The corollary to number three above is to schedule time to do some things together. There is no limit to the number of second honeymoons a couple can have. Shared joys and quiet times deepen into memories. Memories are what life is made of. Try some new experiences together. There ought to be time for tennis, golf, crafts, hobbies, riding, travel, talk, gardening, a leisurely cup of coffee or tea or an early evening walk.

5. Keep up the courtship. Tears came to the eyes of most middle-aged couples when they heard Tevye in *Fiddler on the Roof.* After twenty-five years of marriage he sings, "Do you love me?"

We need to be told over and over in so many ways. We need to tell it over and over in ways that show that it is not just routine. Even on a minister's salary, there are a thousand little things by which one can tell his wife that she is beautiful to him or that a wife can reaffirm her feelings for her husband.

In *Love Poems for the Very Married*, Lois Wyse writes,

> *"You never made*
> *A lamp base out of a Cracker Jack box,*
> *An extra room out of an unused closet*
> *Or a garden out of a pile of clay*
> *All you ever made was*
> *A woman out of me." (Wyse)*

The young gal on water skis or the one who bounces across the commercial in a sexy way is considered the ultimate image of femininity while the woman of fifty who has devoted years to the careful study of how to make her husband feel wonderful is judged to be old. While by Madison Avenue standards she may be judged to be unattractive, it is not the case for those who continue their courtship.

DON'T DRINK TO THAT

Alcohol is another plague of middle-age. Here again, there are few facts to document it as a problem of ministers but many of us can list friends for whom it is not a statistic. Major changes have taken place in the attitude of the church toward drinking. At one point. Methodist ministers according to the book of discipline were forbidden to drink. Someone has said that this change has been to allow "Presbyterians to drink . . . in public." Perhaps the best thing to do here is to raise a danger flag for those who might be caught in the middle-age holding pattern. Alcohol and flying don't mix. If you are up in the air about your future, your marriage or yourself, get your feet on the ground before you try to resolve the problem with liquid refreshment.

By god, it's *my* answer!

ME, ME, ME

Misery does not need company but misery tends to want an audience. We will talk to anyone who is willing to listen and even to some who aren't so willing. This is natural and no doubt it is therapeutic. It may help in providing some perspectives and in reaffirming a sense of worth. But it also focuses on frustration and anxieties. Preoccupation with one's own problems is another side-effect. To offset this, we will need to listen. We need to listen to our spouse and to our children. We need to move out to help

Of course no problem is too *big* or too *small* for us to discuss, J.C. It's all of your *mediocre* problems that are a pain in the neck!

someone else with his or her adolescence, youth, "middles-cence" or old-age. Part of the cure for this disease is the conscious effort to move outside of oneself. Our peer group provides a starting place.

When will the clergy learn? We need each other. How long has it been since you really offered support to another minister? How often do you really share the hurts and frustrations of a neighboring pastor? The answer to many of our own anxieties and uneasiness will lie in the commitments of clergy to provide mutual support. To be pastor, teacher, counselor to each other.

THE SLOUGH OF DESPAIR

Personal frustrations have been the focus of much comment on mid-career "dis-ease." But this is also a period when there are potentials for serious disappointments which are brought upon us by others. More than one middle-aged minister longs for a telephone call from a son in a far country or lays awake nights wondering what went wrong with relationships with sons or daughters who have turned their backs on the church or rejected their parents. Repeated "we-are-sorry-to-inform-you" letters can develop deep skepticism about the church and its systems which show little sensitivity to human feelings. Whatever happened to friendships? There are jobs which disappoint and friends who fail and forget, official boards which are unresponsive, salaries which just won't stretch, and hoped-for recognition which doesn't materialize. All of these compound to buffet and baffle the clergyperson who is questioning his or her competency and commitment.

There is no quick egress from the slough of disappointment but one must get out. The biblical understanding of human nature teaches us not to put our ultimate grounds for hope in people or positions or process. When disappointments come, we can find strength in the community of the faithful or in the arms of those we love, but in the last analysis it will need to come from the quiet sustaining confidence in the love of God.

"Have you not known? Have you not heard? . . . They that wait upon the Lord shall renew their strength. They shall mount up with wings like eagles. They shall run and not be weary. They shall walk and not faint."

So You'd Like to Leave the Ministry

I f there are times when you think you are in the wrong vocation, you are not alone. One of the common experiences identified with "middlescence" is centered on one's life work. Is it significant? Is it fulfilling? Is it worth it?

My contacts would lead me to believe that ministers are especially susceptible to this feeling. It may be due to the very nature of our calling or it may be due to the lack of clear signals as to "how we are doing." Among those who responded to a questionnaire, more than one-half indicated they have given serious thought to leaving the ministry. Breathes there a person (clergy type) with soul so dead, who never to himself has said, "There must be a better way?"

It is my conviction that a transition to non-church related employment ought to be an option for all ministers. Nor should such a move carry any stigma or guilt. Those who responded to the above questionnaire were invited to a conference to explore the possibilities, the processes and the pitfalls of a second career. After some uneasy jokes about "ministers anonymous," a degree of trust developed and the conversations became serious. The time was spent talking about the job market, how one goes about seeking other employment and the particular problems of ministers in making this kind of a choice. I am not aware of anyone who used this knowledge to make a change. However, I'm sure that each of us is wiser to the ways of the job market. This in and of itself is a detriment to moving.

Any decision for a clergyperson to change vocations will be a lonely one. Standing by parishioners in their hour of desperate need does not guarantee easy support for a pastor who needs to move. Often a sense of guilt for "leaving the ministry" inhibits conversation even with other pastors. The appearance of a number of articles focusing with almost morbid curiosity on the number of persons who were moving "out into the real world" has made sensitive persons even more hesitant to bare their searchings.

A second career may not be a personally initiated choice. There are indications that a significant number of clergy will be forced to seek other means of employment. In spite of stories about the large number of clergy who are "demitting" the ministry, there is no shortage of trained, ordained personnel. The competition for vacant pulpits is sobering. One study of ministers who left the church for other employment indicated that they were forced to do so. (Jud) Desiring to move to another parish, and finding none available, they reluctantly accepted other work.

Since 1966, a group called "Bearings for Re-establishment" has existed to assist church professionals of all faiths in career transition. Originally, they concentrated on providing food, clothing, housing and transportation for those looking for employment. One ex-nun who spent nine days sleeping in Grand Central Station and eating only Metrecal is typical of their first clients. Located at 235 East 49th Street, New York, N.Y. 10017, they provide counsel in exploring career alternatives and even a placement bureau.

A DO-IT-YOURSELF REPORT CARD
One clear prerequisite for changing vocations is an appraisal of

one's vocational strengths and weaknesses. It is one thing to aspire to First Church by First National, the Presidency of Co-ed College or Director of Out-yonder Larger Parish. It may be another thing to have the combination of skills, temperament and friends to secure the coveted position. Knowing what one has to offer is basic.

There are helps in this process of self-evaluation. Each of these may vary in technique and usefulness. The key is *self-evaluation.* Each approach will raise questions but you must supply the answers and the evaluation. There are some ''do-it-yourself kits'' which will assist by providing a format and a process for an individual who feels disciplined enough to complete the process alone. These will help separate those things in past jobs which were liked from those which were disliked, those which were satisfying from those which were a drag. The more elaborate process will involve using agency or individual guidance. This will include testing, psychological interviews and counseling. If a person is serious about making a vocational change, he or she ought to use the services of one of the many Career Counseling Centers designed for ministers. The cost may seem high but it is a small investment considering all of the concurrent family and personal adjustment which will be involved. Even if the decision is against a change, it enables a person to have a better idea of direction and values.

Career Counseling Centers are not employment agencies. They can only help by asking the right questions, providing some objective information and by being a good sounding board and by facilitating decision-making. To this degree they are limited. Their best chance of being ''helpful'' is to make one content to stay-put vocationally. This in and of itself is valuable, even if it is a limitation.

WHAT TURNS YOU ON

An executive was recently counseling a minister who was contemplating a change in vocation. ''What you really want to

Part of our problem is, we're overqualified! The other part is, nobody seems to know for what!

be," he said, "is basically answered in the heart and not in the head."

Here again the dilemma for knowing what we want to do is easier said than done. It is often just the heart of our frustration. One approach is to identify what we don't want to do. It may be that we are allowing what we don't like to force us out of what we are doing. Other alternatives will not necessarily change that. There will be something about most every job that we don't like. A sense of realism can prevent impulsive judgements about alternatives. A friend recently discovered in two months as a sports writer that journalism had the same pressure he had sought to leave behind in the parish.

Still beyond job satisfactions, there needs to be a bank of skills. Lawrence J. Peter has parlayed the idea of the "Peter Principle" into a household word. He repeatedly illustrates how someone moves into a job which is beyond his level of competence and is unhappy. Professional counseling may not prevent this but it is worth the expense to get some objective evaluation.

HOW FREE ARE YOU?

At best change of career will involve some rather radical adjustments. With some it will be a matter of judgement whether or not the price is worth it. It is important to explore what sacrifices will be required. Here are some questions that should be pondered.

1. Do you have a second marketable skill? It is unfortunate that even after seven years of college, most ministers are not equipped to transfer into the secular job market without some additional training. Clergypersons seem most often to move from the ministry to teaching, counseling and service-oriented positions. This, of course, might not be your field or skill. But it is important to know what one has to offer and what the demand is for that ability.

2. If retraining is essential to accomplish a second career, do you have the financial resources to obtain the credentials necessary for the position sought? It is true that there are a number of scholarship-type aids which are available. However, many scholarships were established assuming that the recipient would have few responsibilities. The stipend is not normally designed to support both parents and offspring in college at the same time.

3. Can you deal with the emotional adjustment of not being "the pastor" or being surrounded by a community of concerned per-

Do you ever get the feeling you're not even good at what you're good at?

sons and where you have some status? Can you handle the matter of demitting the ministry or the family pressures? I recently heard of one former priest who wears clerical garb when he visits his family because of the stigma on his parents if the neighbors knew that he had left the church.

4. Is your family "locked in" to a geographic area or a style of life which limit your opportunities? If you move, it is important that the new position brings fulfillment and satisfaction. Taking any old job will not satisfy the unrest in the minister. Are you tied to financial obligations which pressure you to go or stay?

5. Do you really have a good reason for changing? Is it one with which you can live if the move turns out to be a mistake? One of the most difficult office visits for me is with former pastors who have taken secular employment and want to "get back into the ministry." It is just not all that easy.

6. If you are convinced that you need to change vocations, must you do it immediately or can you wait for the "right" thing? Ministers have a strong sense of worth tied up in their jobs. There may be times when a quick move is essential for personal integrity, but if one is to move, it is better to plan in that direction rather than announce on impulse that you are resigning.

WHAT OTHERS HAVE DONE

Obviously none of the above obstacles is insurmountable. In my own experience, I am aware of the following courses of action by those who have left the ministry at mid-career. Some acted on their own initiative. Others felt forced to do so for a variety of reasons. Some are happy with their choices and some are bitter toward themselves and toward the church.

1. A second career. It would be impossible to list all of the kinds of occupations which have been chosen. Here is a sample: college teaching, high school counseling, real estate, county health, county welfare, juvenile parole officer, insurance, personnel, business management, banking, golf pro, school administration. The opportunities are related to skills and training. The satisfactions are related to the interest and values of the individual.

2. Sticking it out. There is not quite the interest in relocating out of the ministry as there was a few years ago. It may well be that an examination of the alternatives has indicated that the grass is not all that much greener beyond the gate. I remember sitting in the office of a former pastor who was working in an urban renewal project. Three times during my short visit his secretary brought the same paper in for some minor correction. It had to do with how he had charged his time for one of his activities. We joked about how this kind of "Mickey Mouse" in the church had driven him up the walls.

Certainly something as serious as changing professional careers should require careful evaluation of the environment into which the move is proposed. We may not like everything where we are but it could be worse.

3. Vocational renewal. This is more than just sticking it out. It is trying to bring some new elements into the situation which transforms our attitude and perhaps our skills in answering it. The Doctor of Ministry program has done this for some pastors. Being able to take a specific aspect of parish life which is of particular interest and make an indepth study with the help of outside experts has been rewarding. Seeing problems as opportunities and working them through to resolution gives both relief and satisfaction. The D. Min. program also requires seminars with others working on similar projects giving a support community which results in the ability to "stay in there."

4. Finding a secondary interest. This can be directly related to the responsibilities of the pastor or a personal interest on the side. One very able and yet thwarted pastor found that he was being called upon to do more and more counseling. He enrolled at the university in some courses assuming that he would go into the school system as a guidance counselor when he had the proper credentials. The classroom work was stimulating. The discipline of study gave his pastoral ministry new effectiveness. He found

You think it's easy . . . being subservient all the time?

such new interest in what he was doing that he stayed in that parish with renewed enthusiasm.

One of the side benefits of the additional education was that it provided him with a second marketable skill. He no longer felt "trapped" in the parish. He moved with a great deal more confidence and freedom.

This secondary interest could be in the field of a hobby or community activity. Most pastors have trouble with this. Our very motivation to the ministry puts a premium on service: things to be done. The list of needs is as inexhaustible as it is exhausting. As a result, time has not been given to do non-church oriented community activities or for developing hobbies that divert our emotions. There are pastors who have literally been saved be-

I finally found the secret to keeping my head down! I pray!

cause they developed interests which were so absorbing that they were able to get out from under the pressures and tensions of parish demands. Did you ever consider acting in the little theater, playing in the local symphony, building an airplane or sailboat, going back-packing, whittling? Each of these has been a redeeming emotional outlet for a pastor that I know.

5. Back to school. One very acceptable and frequent move is to return to seminary for an advanced degree. There are some plus factors for this if you can afford it. Unless you have stayed up-to-date in reading and self-directed study, it may be a time for re-tooling. There have been changes in theology and a whole growing body of liturgy and worship. Not even preaching is the same.

Hello, dial-a-prayer? I'd like to audition!

Whether it is for a degree or just for a year's refresher, a new parish will be faced with updated skills and fresh commitments.

The danger, of course, is to find a job upon the completion of the study program. Competition for pastors will not have diminished. An advanced degree, especially if it carries a specialization or additional skills, may well offset this by making one more competent to handle a wider variety of opportunities.

6. Move within the church. There are a wide variety of positions within the church which provide alternatives to some of the frustrations which may exist in the generalized role of pastor. A "specialist" on a staff of a larger church in administration, education or calling is one set of possibilities. There are a number of ministers who have found their niche as a team member when they had been harried as *the* pastor. Chaplaincies for hospitals and institutions have attracted those who prefer the counseling and supporting ministries of personal relationships. Jokes abound

about those who have "left the ministry" to be administrators within the life and structures of the church.

This list is intended only to suggest that there are others who have been ahead of you at the "holding time of life." They have found a variety of ways of meeting their crisis. There is a way for you.

HOW DOES ONE MAKE THE BREAK

> *Those who have gone the route before, all say the same*
> *thing.*
> *This is how we go about it, when our time has come;*
> *We procrastinate,*
> *that's what we do.*
> *Busy winding things up, we say.*
> *Actually, if the truth were known,*
> *we're hoping for that miracle; you know the one;*
> *that if we just sit tight a little longer,*
> *we won't have to go job-hunting, no*
> *the job will come hunting for us.*
> *Right in the front door, it will come.*
> *But, it doesn't, and of course,*
> *eventually, we realize that time*
> *and money*
> *are beginning to run out.*

Those lines are from *What Color is Your Parachute?* by Richard Nelson Bolles. It is the most comprehensive manual and directory of resources for clergy considering a self-supporting ministry or a second career that is available. If you want to dispel your dreams either by making them a reality or reducing them to fantasy, this book is a place to start. The author examines all of the normal channels and gives the facts on what you can expect

Of course I aspire to greater heights. But, assuming I attained them, what would I have to look forward to?

through friends, executive placement bureaus and personnel departments. It is rather sobering. His conclusion is that the best way is to determine what you want to do and can do well, where you want to work and for what company or organization. He then suggests finding the person who hires for that position and convince him that you have something he needs. Bolles' thesis is that you have the best chance of getting a job not because the prospective employer is going to do you a favor but because you have convinced him that you have the answer to his problems.

Job hunting for persons over fifty-five has its own set of pitfalls. Job hunting for clergy in this age bracket who have limited marketable skills is even more difficult. However, don't be intimidated. It is repeatedly being done successfully. Start by ordering the Bolles' book. Then contact some former pastors who have made the transition. Their first hand experience will be helpful.

Peter Drucker, a respected management consultant, encourages people to be wide open to the possibilities of second careers. He is quoted as saying, "Here I am fifty-eight, and I still don't know what I am going to do when I grow up." (Hall)

THE CAREER DEVELOPMENT COUNCIL

The Career Development Council gives accreditation to a series of centers which are qualified to provide career assessment and counseling services for professional church workers. The following is a list of approved Career Development Council Centers:

Career Development Center
St. Andrew's Presbyterian College
Laurinburg, NC 28352

Career Development Center
Eckerd College
St. Petersburg, FL 33733

Center for the Ministry
7804 Capwell Drive
Oakland, CA 94621

Center for the Ministry
40 Washington Street
Wellesley Hills, MA 02181

Church Career Assessment Center
240 Plant Avenue
Tampa, FL 33606

Counseling Center
Davis and Elkins College
Elkins, WV 26241

Lancaster Career Development
Center
561 College Avenue
P. O. Box 1529
Lancaster, PA 17604

Mid-Atlantic Career Center
Suite 725
1500 Massachusetts Avenue, NW
Washington, DC 20005

Midwest Career Development
Center
66 East 15th Avenue
Columbus, OH 43201

Midwest Career Development
Center
800 West Belden Ave.
Chicago, IL 60614

New England Career Development Center
40 Washington Street
Wellesley Hills, MA 02181

North Central Career Development Center
3000 Fifth Street, N.W.
New Brighton, MN 55112

Northeast Career Center
40 Witherspoon Street
Princeton, NJ 08540

Western Career Development
Center
109 Seminary Road
San Anselmo, CA 94960

Career Development Council
Room 760
475 Riverside Drive
New York, NY 10027

Southwest Career Development
Center
Suite 712
2723 Avenue "E" East
Arlington, TX 76011

A Smorgasbord For Growth

Personal growth and renewal reclaim middle-age. It is true that time will eventually resolve our frustrations but most of us are too impatient for that. Middle-age is a period for new ventures. We ought to have enough self-confidence and courage to experiment. Don't allow some amusement on the part of friends to deter your harmonica lessons, or your aspirations to be a writer, or the idea of getting your Master's Degree be hampered by a few raised eyebrows or "you gotta be kidding."

It is so important that we continue to grow professionally and individually. The changes in our world are so massive that we become obsolete by inertia. One is no longer educated for the job, he must be continually educated on the job. Stagnation is the best feeder of the malaise. To grow is both to show and generate hope and purpose. To learn is to conquer limitations. To expand one's vision and develop one's abilities in mid-career is to enhance the significance of the last third of life. "Doctors agree on the therapeutic value of nearly all new skills acquired in late middle-age." (Ellis) The following is a cafeteria of suggestions for growth. Each person must "pick and choose." If you have tried several, pick a new one and try again.

APPETIZERS

1. Conferences. There are innumerable short conferences happening in your community, at a near-by college or university or around the country which will give exposure to ideas and areas where you might later want to do further study or reading. Here is just a partial list of such events which have come across my desk in just the last few months: A seminar on discipleship and worship; a conference on planning for retirement; bridge lessons; tennis and golf instructions; safe pilot school; invest in real estate; dog obedience training; gardening for fun; patio cooking; art for the beginner; rock-hound trips. The weekend edition of most papers carry an extensive listing. All of us receive such notices through the mail.

2. Read some books. My observation is that there is a direct ratio between a pastor's effectiveness and his reading habits. His effectiveness has a direct bearing on his self-image and ability to handle both himself and his work. Yet it is startling to discover that Baptist ministers read on the average of three books a year and United Presbyterians manage only five. It is true that books are expensive but there are alternatives to buying everything that is published. Trade with fellow clergy (not just of your own denomination). There are several persons I know who are doing good current reading whom I frequently ask to recommend the best book that they have read in the last six months or a year. Libraries are willing to get on loan almost any book you want. Belonging to a regular study group will help to keep you abreast of new books and will give the added insights of discussion. To have this kind of exchange with your peer group will take you off the spot of being expected to be the leader of every discussion in your own parish.

3. Take a day off. This should not be related to your work. Visit the closest museum or art gallery. Hear some good music. Go for a hike. Play tennis. Once in a while, this time should be spent

Can I talk with you for a minute, dear, before you start to think?

alone although it is a good way to share time with one's spouse. In fact, she or he may be able to introduce you to some areas and resources of your community of which you were unaware.

4. Think. IBM doesn't have a patent on this. Tournier tells of a friend who gave up his medical practice to become a "teacher-of-how-to-think." He said leaders need to grasp problems and ideas thoroughly rather than just reacting with stop-gap measures. "Between their adversaries running them down and their supporters flattery, they do not know to whom they may turn for objective debate on their problems." (Tournier) It would be particularly helpful for ministers to have this kind of objective reflective moments.

THE ENTREES

1. Study leave. The evolvement of programs of continuing educa-

tion in the ministry has been haphazard but interesting. As a Presbyterian, I have watched Presbyterians work to have a two-week study leave plus financial help included in each call of a pastor. It is now almost universal. However, there is no program to urge people to take advantage of this opportunity. I am not aware of any radical shift in the continuing education of clergy since the advent of this provision. Those who were interested had been finding ways of doing it. Those who didn't feel so motivated are not now doing it just because the time is available.

A study leave differs from a conference in that there is adequate time for some serious study and growth. Hopefully it might be related to some career development goals. The emergence of the Doctor of Ministry program may give some depth to this provision. Several of the seminaries have significant summer programs as do centers like Ghost Ranch, Montreat, Kirkridge and others.

2. Vacations. This is a good time to do something other than travel, play, paint the house or visit one's parents. There are more interesting values to be had in spending the month in another parish. Volunteer to fill the pulpit of a friend in a different type of church. Tell him you want the works not just the Sunday preaching bit. Meet with the committees. Teach a class. Attend the women's association and youth events. You will be surprised at what you will learn both as to how much better they are doing some things than are you and vice versa. This might be arranged in an area where you can learn something of another culture: minority, urban, rural. It should be stimulating enough to be re-creating, and unstructured enough to be fun.

Another use of vacation is to try another job. If you are toying with the idea of secular employment, explore the possibilities of a short-term job in that field. Either some of your parishioners or those of a fellow pastor might be able to arrange this for you. It will give you some insights into both a life-style and a work pattern which would be helpful both in decisions about the future

We appreciate your participation in our learning group, Reverend Middy . . . but most of us feel you already *knew* how to sleep!

and how your parishioners live. The extra money might come in handy, too, although if it is done for this purpose, it will probably not be either much of a learning experience or vacation.

3. Form a group for mutual support and study. Jeffrey K. Hadden in *Confusion and Hope: Clergy and Laity and the Church in Transition*, affirms that ministers can support each other. It doesn't happen too often now, he admits, but it has real hope and promise. I have watched one study group in action in my area. They are not always as supportive as they might be but they are a long way ahead of those pastors who don't belong to such a group. They have had to weather the charges of being a clique and the whims of a variety of breakfast chefs, several changes in membership and spotty preparation by those whose turn it is to lead the study. But the fact that it has continued through the years confirms its importance.

Such groups don't just happen. They take effort. But over a period of time, they become real learning centers and most important, they become the base for trust and commitment to help one another cope with his or her task. Hadden says we cannot expect this to be a denominational program. It must be done by those who have the need and the interest. He says, "Organize, divide labor, create reciprocal expectations. Utilize community resources. Build psychic support. Develop the collective strength to purge defense mechanisms and rationalizations, and get on with the work." Could it be that this is why God has made us so different and given to us different skills and approaches? That out of our variety of temperaments and talents we can bring to the church and the world a wider, more effective, more inclusive and hence more Christ-like presence of God?

4. Write for publication. There can be a great deal of satisfaction when one sees something in print that he has written. One bookstore owner in responding to the question, "What do people look for when they come into your store?" replied, "Their own book."

There is more of a market for written material than most of us realize. *The Writers Market* which is probably available in your library will give some suggestions as to the possibilities for selling written material. It also tells what is expected, the rate of pay and addresses of publishers. There are courses in many community colleges and universities on creative writing. A publisher's consultant has indicated that creative writing is one of the last remaining uncomputerized fields.

5. Personal discipline. Is there a conflict between creativity and discipline or are they related? Is spontaneity limited by routine? Does planning preclude freedom for uninhibited response? The new generation emphasizes the sensitivity to the present and our freedom to appreciate and enjoy its wonder and promise. It is rebellious against the oughts and responsibilities. Most of us have

been used to a more rigid and defined way of life. A style which seeks to control both our environment and ourselves. I'm not so sure that these can be set in opposites. It is my experience that discipline can also lead to freedom, and freedom to creativity. It often takes some discipline to get out of bed but the discipline to do so will give me the freedom to do some other things which I really want to do, and to respond to people and events which otherwise would be cut out of my life just by a shortage of time. Personal discipline is a guide through the maze of "middlescence" and it might well be the prescription to renewal.

My own life has been enriched by a rather simple four faceted discipline. Each weekday morning when I am home (well, almost every one) I get up an hour before breakfast to do three things:

Take some exercise such as those of the Canadian Air Force or the President's Physical Fitness Council. This takes 10-12 minutes.

Followed by a cup of coffee and a period of reading which stretches my spirit. It may be Bible or devotional writings. (My prayer time comes later with my wife.)

Spend the remaining time until breakfast either reading or writing.

The fourth aspect of the discipline is to try consciously to do something for someone during the day which I would not normally have done. I find this the easiest to overlook. Each day, therefore, I try to do something to grow in body, spirit, mind and sensitivity to others.

This routine does not contain the possibilities for salvation but I believe that it does help to make me a more authentic person, more aware of my own needs and more alert to those with whom I will come in contact during the day. This is not a variation on the old approach: every day in every way I am getting better and better. It is, rather, the realization that the body, mind and spirit need to be stretched if they are to grow.

6. Build your self-confidence. This can be a gimmick. I remember a speaker at a luncheon club when I was in my first parish. He was speaking on the subject of building confidence. The only thing that I can remember was that he advised putting metal clips on the heels of your shoes. This was supposed to command attention when you walked into a room and therefore give assurance that you were noticed. The first Sunday in which I walked up that uncarpeted aisle at the church in my new cleats made me very self-conscious but not self-confident. The click of my heel at each step seemed to echo through the sanctuary like a tattoo on the snare drum.

No person who has spent twenty-plus years in the ministry is without some ego reinforcing experience. In dealing with minis-

It never fails . . . around the house I'm a moron! Put on my robe, step into the pulpit, and by god I'm *it!*

terial relations "problems" in local congregations, I have yet to meet with a committee which did not say positive things about their pastor. They may have been convinced that he ought to move for his good and/or theirs. But they recognized his good qualities and used phrases like: "He's a good preacher, a sensitive pastor, knows the community or relates to youth."

These qualities ought to be cultivated and appreciated. They are the places where we can reach down and touch a solid place to stand while seeking to grow in other ways. Confidence in one area will help give confidence in others. Confidence breeds confidence as the saying goes. You are better than you think you are.

Cleats on the heels aren't all just noise. Changing one's style of dress or growing a beard does have an effect on self-image. The degree that this gives assurance or enhances one's confidence will vary. Do you have the nerve to try?

7. Formal education. After seven years, who needs it? We do! And what is exciting is the number and varieties of opportunities. In almost every community, there are courses in adult education. The rise of the community college has brought continuing education within reach geographically and financially of almost everyone. Extension classes from the university can or will fill the gap. The catalogues show things ranging from fly-tying to world events. A dean of the night school at one local college has said to me, "If we don't have what you want, help us get the students (from your church?) and we will find the teacher and add the class to the curriculum."

8. Teach a class. Here again, community colleges have open doors to possible growth. There are a number of ministers who have made a contribution to the community and found an outlet for frustrations by teaching one or more classes. They need not all be in the field of religion. Undergraduate degrees or advanced study may give competence in other areas. I am aware of clergy teaching comparative religion, philosophy, history and math.

Teaching itself is learning. Preparation forces a searching for contemporary information. Teaching pushes beyond lectures to other ways of communication which may have carry-over values into the church. The interchange between student and student and between student and teacher sharpens one's perceptions and concepts.

9. Take a smaller church. This sounds like a poor way to grow. But I know of several ministers who felt that the administrative pressures of a larger congregation were so demanding on their time that they were unable to find the time for study and for experimenting with new forms of worship and teaching. They knew that it takes effort to change and they were too pooped after a day's activity to give time to creative preparations.

There's *no* business like *show* business . . .!

THE DESSERT

After one has taken a look at some of the more serious prods to growth, there are still some lighter activities which can have their own renewal quotient.

1. Develop a hobby. Creative use of leisure time is an art and not an inherited trait. We are told that ministers are so tied up in their "Protestant work ethic" that they have forgotten how to enjoy themselves. Hobbies should be enjoyable. They are also a source

of freedom. Many can look to the excitement and diversion of hobbies as the great "unwinder."

But hobbies, like horses, should be chosen with care. They can be as demanding as our work. They can be expensive. They can be frustrating.

2. Spend some time with friends. The older one gets, the more important friends become. Friendships grow and help us to grow. Accepting, open friendships provide, next to the family, the most fertile opportunities for serious discussions of those things which are more important. Time can be taken to think through ideas and to clarify positions. There is a depth of understanding which is crucial to our stability. We need each other.

Building Support Systems

Those caught in the "dis-ease" of middle-age need our support even as we need theirs. This chapter is intended for those families, congregations and denominations where there is an awareness of the debilitating effects of "middlescence" and they want to help. John Donne needs to be updated. For no person is an island. No man stands alone.

God, for this very reason, set us in families and calls us into the church. It is not possible to meet the crises of life, of which "middlescence" is one, without the acceptance and support of those we love and those who love us. This growing awareness of dependence may indeed be a major factor in the self-questioning which haunts the person in mid-career. There is, of necessity, a frustration which surrounds the awakening realization of our limitations. One soon learns that he has neither the enthusiasm nor the abilities to do all that he had hoped to do. His horizons seem to be pulling in. One feels "bound in" because he has not kept up with the change or been "plugged in" to the power structures. It is easy to think that one has been unfairly treated because that sought-for position went to someone else.

Ministers who never get a visit from a Pastor-Seeking Committee begin to wonder about themselves. There are those in my area who have received at least a dozen form letters which begin

"Thank you for allowing us to read your dossier. Your qualifications and experiences don't correspond to our job description
. . ." It puts feelings right on the line. If a person is confident of
his or her own ability and knows that the dossier presented
matches the job description, there is only one conclusion. Too
old . . . too old. They were looking for someone younger. Unfortunately, this is often the case.

WHAT THE WIFE CAN DO

This might better be written "What the spouse can do" but by
far most middle-aged ministers are male and this will be one
section of the book where the language acknowledges that fact.

In a study by the United Church of Christ on those who had left
the ministry, the single most important source of support which
men in this vocational crisis felt came from their wives. This was
true of both the control group and those who were being studied.

Dr. Maria Levinson, one of a team at Yale University studying
the effects of middle-age, says they receive letters asking for
help. "Most of the mail we receive is fairly typical. Wives who
write in—from 'the two of us'—on behalf of a husband who
seems to have caught some kind of virus, something which at-
tacks men at mid-life. The wife's initial response is often a kind
of frenzy of mothering. Her husband is sick with this thing and
her question is how can she cure him?" (Scarf)

Dr. Levinson goes on to say she should view it as a stage in the
developmental process not as a kind of flu. It is a time when a
serious transition is being made which involves feelings of unset-
tlement, and sometimes turmoil.

Dr. Daniel Levinson, Maria's husband and director of the study, says that the wife has two responsibilities: to herself and to
her husband. "To help her husband," he says, "she has to be
able to join him in his problems. It's not enough for her to find
new ways to look nice, or to try to be sexier. She has to recognize
the despair he may be feeling, and she has to be willing, for

Chin up! Shoulders back! Chest out! Stomach in! Now . . . go
get 'em, Tiger!!

example, to let her husband tell her how lousy he thinks their
marriage is—which may be painful for her.'' The Levinsons point
out that the problem may be both initiated or caused by the wife
either wittingly or because of the struggles which she herself is
undergoing.

When a wife recognizes and wants to identify with her husband, there are some specific things which she can do or not do.

1. She can reinforce his good feelings about himself and his abilities. If it is sincere, a husband draws a great deal of his ego

satisfactions from his wife. She is the closest to him and the one he trusts the most.

2. There are times when he will want to be alone. When a man feels disappointed by what he has done with his life and is disturbed by his own inability to cope with relationships, he may not want to talk. He may well be humiliated enough not to want to show the hurt and even the sense of rejection which he may have suffered from co-workers or family. He may even want to be where he can cry, and it is hardly a time to try to get him to change the culture's image that men don't cry.

3. If she understands this is a stage of life and not the end, she may be able to take a more accepting stance. Overlook some actions or words, which to challenge would only intensify the internal conflict raging just under the surface of his emotions. Read together *The Intimate Enemy* by George Bach.

4. Encourage him to venture out in new areas of growth. After all of these years, you should know him well enough to guide him into some experiences which reaffirm life and his own sense of worth.

5. In spite of Dr. Levinson's comment that it is not enough just to try to be sexier, certainly it is not useful to try to be less attractive or less loving. If, as some studies indicate, impotency is often a symptom of this malaise, it is surely important to be attractive in his eyes. Impotency is one of those cyclical systems which feeds itself. Estrangement breeds estrangement. Impotency breeds impotency. Acceptance, understanding and loving can be factors in rehabilitation.

This decade of unrest and uneasiness, of emotional and physical changes does not need to be a threat to the marriage or to either partner. The better that they understand the changes which are taking place, the better they can handle them. It can well be

No sermons, please!

the beginning of a new and deeper relationship and the basis for stronger and more profound understandings in the future.

WHAT THE CONGREGATION CAN DO

Much of the minister's unrest will be focused on the congregation. He will assume that his relationship with them (or lack of it) will be the cause of his "dis-ease." If he has grown stale, they didn't respond to his leadership. If he is harried, a change of pastorates would make all things look new. If he thinks himself overworked, that new church with an associate pastor or a larger staff would be just the thing. If there are financial problems in the

You've *told* me all your problems, Miss Grady! For a change
of pace, why don't I tell you *mine?*

family, a larger salary (which he doesn't feel that his parish is
about to give him) will solve all of his problems.

Now obviously, he has "superoversimplification." But that is
not the point. The question is not how you can straighten him out
but how you can help him. He will come to reality in time if the
congregation can be understanding and supportive.

It needs to be said that being a minister is not an easy task.
There is a continual conflict between what a person is and his
commitments and faith. There are a wide variety of pressures,
some internal and some external. He needs acceptance.

Here are some specifics:

1. He needs help to be an authentic person. As a preacher he finds
some want to be challenged, others prefer to be comforted. As a

But, dammit Ruby, it makes me feel with it or something, to cuss in front of a preacher!

teacher he is expected to relate the gospel to the world—without offending anyone of course. As a pastor, he learns he should call—but not too often. He must relate to youth but does he need to grow a beard? The assurance that he is loved as a person will give him a freedom of movement which will allow him to know that he can grow, and indeed may grow more by staying with his parish. A person who is supported through these kinds of times will develop into a wiser, stronger, more mature pastor and his congregation will benefit by that growth.

2. His salary should be reviewed annually. Peter Drucker points out, "There is no more powerful disincentive, no more effective bar to motivation, than dissatisfaction over one's pay compared to that of one's peers." This is always a touchy point. If the pastor is struggling with bills or frustrated over inability to assist the children with college expenses, it eats away at his self-esteem further contributing to his self-criticism. Here he is at the height of his career in skill and productivity and can't pay his bills or buy his wife a new dress or take that trip to visit the new grandchildren. It is really a tragedy that so many congregations fail to keep pace in their salaries with either the cost of living or a family's increasing needs. So the person leaves in order to get enough money just to meet basic costs. Invariably that congregation when they are seeking a replacement must pay more to the new man than they had been paying.

3. He needs to be shown that he is loved. From time to time there should be something special done for him and his family. This doesn't need to be a trip to the Holy Land. A card of thanks, a bouquet of flowers, something from a garden, a kind word, two tickets to a football game, a piece of artwork. If he is doing any job at all, he will get enough knocks to keep him humble and enough blarney to keep him suspicious.

4. Deal with conflict. Where new ideas are circulating and where the gospel is at work, there will be conflict. Not all of us have the same needs or the same understandings of what the church should be and do. One should approach these differences with openness and trust. One should assist the pastor in seeing that they are faced. They may not all be resolved and part of our continued growth in the faith is due to the agitation which keeps the soil of our lives loose enough that growth can happen.

. . . and I feel certain I could meditate even more efficiently with a slight raise, amen!

5. When a congregation is seeking a pastor, full consideration should be given to some persons over fifty. My observation after 20 years of administration is that age is not the key factor in a person's effectiveness as a minister. This isn't to say that generalizations about age characteristics are without some validity. There can be a kind of freshness and optimistic enthusiasm of youth which gives life to a whole congregation. A minister in his or her late forties may well have the combination of experience and vitality which puts him in the prime of his life. But there are places where maturity and good judgment may be more important to the life of the church. Some of the greatest contributions to society and the church have been made by persons "over fifty," indeed, over 65. The Scriptures paint the dramatic story of the trials of Job and remind us of the value of a seasoned life. "Wisdom is with the aged, and understanding in length of days."

WHAT CAN THE DENOMINATION DO?

This section is not being directed to the "decision makers" in the denominational structures as a program for pastors in middle-

. . . and please don't let it get out that Billy Graham is eight years *older* than me!

age. However, there are some things which official groups can do as part of the everyday system of support.

1. First, encourage pastors to develop their own mutual support groups. Any program to do so will probably not meet with overwhelming success. There is a kind of needed "ad-hocracy" about such groups. Assist in some experimentation. Be a catalyst in bringing some groups together. This should not require a big program budget.

2. Recognize middle-age as a time of crisis in the ministry. There have been a number of seminars designed for pastors and spouses in mid-career. Those who have attended have found them most helpful.

Including both husband and wife in such conferences recognizes the mutuality of both the unrest and of the resolution. If these are held on a small area basis, the costs would be minimal.

I couldn't give up the ministry! I don't know that I have suffi-
cient qualifications to be just a person!

3. Offer opportunities to retool as a way of moving out of the
ministry. Much attention is given to preparation for ministry.
Seminary training is encouraged and supported. If a person has
twenty years in the pastorate, why not help him or her in transition into another vocation? Peter Drucker indicates that people at
this age ought to give thought to a second career as a way of
keeping alert and growing. With modern educational techniques,
it ought to be possible to retrain ministers into positions of service and esteem. We are always wanting to make an impact on
business or government or education. What about assisting some
theologically trained person to move into these fields as our
"missionaries." If, as indicated, there will be need to move clergy into secular employment, why not capitalize on it and conserve their dedication for the church?

4. Work for the removal of the stigma on persons who leave the
active or ordained ministry. This is a hard one. We are so in-
grained with the sense of holiness that surrounds the clergy. To

My cup may be full, bishop, but it *never* runneth over!

give up ordination is kind of like spitting in the face of God. Why should this be? In Protestantism a person is ordained for function. We are all ministers. If a person no longer is performing that function, why should he or she not give up ordination? One Presbyterian minister told me how difficult it was for him to make this break. What really bothered him, however, was that when he did demit and was told that he would be given a letter of membership to any congregation of his choice, not a single pastor in the presbytery invited him to join with them.

5. Dr. Levinson thinks that society should use persons in middle-age as "mentors" to younger persons. (Levinson) A mentor is someone usually eight to ten years older who has some expert

skills or experience to share with younger men. For the younger person, the mentor represents a period of his own development. It is someone who is a friend, who has accomplished some of the things which he himself would like to accomplish. Dr. Braxton McKee indicates that the mentor becomes in some sense a parent figure for the younger person, helping him through a stage in his early adult development.

These are just a few glimpses into an area where the church has yet to discover the many ways in which it can reinforce, conserve and utilize the wisdom and energy of those ministers who are drifting and desiring to be used.

On Making Decisions

D ecisions are never easy. Yet life is a series of choices. Some are relatively unimportant. Some have ramifications into every other aspect of life. Reflecting on the consequence of earlier decisions is a popular game of "middlescence." "I should have" or "We should have" begins too many sentences. Superficially analyzing past judgements will probably not be too productive. In fact it may even militate against making any decisions at all.

If one has difficulty making decisions, this trait may come to real dominance in later years. There are persons who are almost immobilized by the inability to make decisions. The more that is known about a subject the more complicated is an answer. And with maturity, comes the experience that few important choices are simple.

However, maturity also brings some clarification as to what is really important to us. As quoted earlier, Erikson says we should know by now who and what we care for.

This period forces us to clarify our goals. What information there is would indicate that few ministers have clearly articulated long-term career goals. Part of the vagueness of the "middle-age blahs" is the lack of criteria for measuring how important one's life and its accomplishments have been. There are some basic conflicts between the values of service and love which the world never comprehends or accepts and the uses of power which it understands. Society's way to measure "success" does not collate with faithfulness to conscience or obedience to Christ's will. "Advancement" calculated by size of salary always leaves a minister uneasy. Service seen in terms of numbers in the congregation never quite satisfies the question of depth and growth of persons. These concepts are not as precise and measurable as dollars or statistics.

The Vocational Agency of the United Presbyterian Church has been experimenting with a tool called Pastoral Development Profile. It is designed to help a pastor evaluate his or her ministry. Eight areas of competence are defined. It contains 27 scales with 5 levels of performance in each which allows an individual to rate personal proficiency in the skills related to professional performance in those areas. Such a process enables a minister to identify places where growth is needed. It is assumed that it is then possible to develop a plan for improving competence in those aspects of ministry.

Tournier insists "Our life, then, has a meaning for us when we have a definite goal, when we struggle to attain it, when we concentrate on the efforts it calls for, when we face obstacles and accept sacrifices. Of course, it is not yet the total meaning of life. It is a provisional meaning, but it is a valid one." (*Learn to Grow Old*)

For the clergy, certain claims or goals do integrate meaning and activity, purpose and performance. But seldom are these goals and claims systematically defined and reviewed. The experience of a Career Counseling Center can be of real help but unfortunately centers have been seen almost exclusively for crisis evaluation and reflection. This kind of values clarification is useful to those at all stages of career growth and especially for those pondering radical changes in job direction.

The experience of committees reading dossiers is that they are too general. The writer is attempting to present himself in the broadest terms in hopes that something will spark with the reader. The image that often comes through is of someone who

Seek ye first the kingdom . . . evasive bugger that it is!

pressed hope that the reader will make the decision for the writer?

The following section is an attempt to help clergy deal with the matters of decision making at forty-nine plus or minus ten.

HOW DO YOU KNOW GOD'S WILL?

1. A qualification must preface any answer given this question. We never really and completely know God's will. That is one dimension of faith. We must also acknowledge that much harm has been done by those who have claimed to be doing the will of God. But our faith would have us believe that we can approxi-

mate his will. That we are justified in seeking it. He has never left us without some knowledge of himself. He has revealed himself to men in all ages. "In the past God spoke to our ancestors many times and in many ways through the prophets, but in these last days, he has spoken to us through his Son."

Our best way to know his will is to know him. This again, is never foolproof. But I can be more confident of knowing how my wife will react, what her "mind" is on a particular subject because I have lived with her for twenty-five years. We should be more confident of our understanding of the mind or will of God because of our closeness to him through our ministry.

We can be assured that his will is consistent with his revelation of himself as one who gave himself that the world might through Christ have life in abundance. If our vision of his will for us is not loving and good, we can be suspicious that it is not his will.

2. We also know that his will is consistent with what he has led us to know about ourselves. He has given experience and talents which Scripture would have us believe we should use. There are, no doubt, dramatic times when God wants us to junk the past to take on something new and untried. Schweitzer, who at the height of a career in theology, left it for one as a medical missionary in Africa. We must be sensitive to such possibilities. My observation is that there is more apt to be continuity than discontinuity in our experiences. What we know about ourselves, limited as that may be, is a factor in knowing what God would have us do. Our skills and experiences are some of those things which we bring to His service. There is a stewardship of whom we are as well as of what we have.

3. The voice of the church is another way in which we know the will of God. This is not to claim that the church won't make mistakes. The constitution of my own denomination acknowledges the fallibility of the institution. But if the church is the body of Christ, then the voice of the church is the voice of Christ. We need to listen with seriousness. Our service of installation calls

I occasionally hear the voice of God, invariably followed by a commercial!

upon the pastor elect, "God has called you through the church to a special service. You know who we are and what we believe . . ."

It is not always easy to believe that God works through the clergy-relocation processes. When one must initiate having his dossier sent to a pastor-seeking committee, the feeling of a "call" is overshadowed by an awareness of process. A call seems to imply that the job seeks the person. The relocation process in vogue almost necessitates the person seek the job. Without deprecating that feeling, you might remember that Isaiah volunteered (sent in his dossier) when God made a need known to him. The impact of that story would lead us to believe that he felt called.

4. He calls us through needs. Unfortunate as it is, some of the most difficult pastorates are unable to "afford" veteran leadership. They are marginal fields because they have had marginal leadership. From time to time a pastor in a larger church, impressed with the need of such a field, makes a dramatic move which has had equally dramatic results.

5. God also speaks through one's own likes and dislikes. This may be a bit more suspect but it is worth remembering that God does not do violence to our own personhood. We have afloat the idea that God's will must involve sacrifice. The more disagreeable the task, surely the more holy it must be. I joke with one of my clergy friends that "he won't take a job unless he has to wear a hair shirt." He has a keenly developed sense of commitment and will tackle jobs which many will walk away from. He feels obligated to work in the difficult places. In this he is not alone. There is in all of us a sense of what Richard Neihbur used to call the "oughtness", a sense of obligation. If we really enjoy doing something we are a bit suspicious that we are serving our own desires and not God's. That may be.

But to what extent does God speak through our preferences? Limitations must always be acknowledged. A Christian life always has a degree of tension between one's will and God's will, but if God has created us with a conscience, with a degree of judgement and with preferences, may not he also speak through them? The pastor who feels "at home on the range" may well do a better ministry in a rural area than accepting a call to an inner

. . . and use me, Lord, in whatever way You, in Your infinite
wisdom, deem suitable . . .preferably with Thursdays off!

city parish. One who has grown up in suburbia may just put one
more jackass in the country if he accepts a town and country
parish.

Psychologists have a concept called rationalization. It is justi-
fying one's actions or preferences with "good reason." Even
allowing for this phenomenon, there is some value in considering
one's desires (preferences) as one way in which God speaks.

This raises the question of setting limits on commitment. Does
the above country pastor have any right to say, "Under no circumstances will I go to the city?" Obviously not, but it is a
temptation that we all have. Our prime commitment is to Jesus
Christ. These helps are to assist in determining what that means
for you. What sacrifices are you really ready to make when you
sense that he is putting his hand upon you?

6. God speaks to me! What audacity! Yet this is the conviction of

Make a wish, but keep it realistic!

those who have sought his will and lived by what they found. One man writes with conviction, "Yes, I believe that God can speak to us and lead us more surely than our wisest thoughts." Or the Psalmist who could testify, "I sought the Lord and afterward I knew. . . ." The belief that this can happen challenges the faith of those who seek earnestly for guidance only to continue in uncertainty. The belief that this can happen results in conflict when friends get opposite readings. Part of our human existence is this seeking, seeking, seeking; the desire for certainty when God calls us to live by faith.

7. Prayer is another channel of learning God's will. This is often offered as a solution when there is nothing left to suggest. But it works! We may not in that moment of quietness get a clear message or have a messenger materialize out of nothing and speak

with authority. But when we do have a practice of regular and thoughtful prayer, it makes a difference in the assurance with which we make our decisions and select our choices. I find my most useful exercise to be reading meaningful prayers of others. This seems to stretch the crevices in my own mind to a broader understanding of what commitment means. To probe the depths of another person's faith makes me more sensitive to my own needs and to the breadth of the gospel and the scope of human response. Too many of my own prayers tend to be intercessory or petition—"God, use me in any way that would be useful to your church, but mainly as a consultant." Prayers of gratitude and thanksgiving, of adoration and awe. These help me to know what might be the will of God—for me.

AN EXERCISE IN DECISION-MAKING

As you are seeking God's will for you during the next years of your ministry, try using the following as a thought stimulator.

1. List the 10 things which you most like to do as a person.
2. List the 10 things which you most like to do as a Christian.
3. List the 10 things which you most like to do as a minister.

Now put a plus (+) before those which you feel that you can do better in the next 10 years than you did in the last 10 years.

Put a minus (−) before those which you don't feel you will be able to do as well in the next ten years as you could in the last 10 years.

Put an "A" in front of those things which you do alone and a "P" before those you do with other persons.

Put an "I" before those items which you do on your own initiative and an "F" in front of those where someone else takes the initiative.

Put a $ in front of those which cost money and an "O" before those which are free or relatively inexpensive.

Put an "R" in front of those which involve risk and an "S" in front of those which are safe.

Now stop and reflect on what you have said about yourself,
your career and your faith.

Complete the following sentences:

1. A Christian

2. The Church should

3. As a minister

4. Retirement can

5. The best thing about middle-age is

6. A book

7. My wife and I

Does this give you any insights into what is important to you?

Now list in order of importance the factors which would affect
your accepting a call to another church. No one is reading over
your shoulder; be honest.

—— Size
—— Salary
—— Opportunities to teach
—— Nature of the community
—— Difficulty or challenge of task
—— Geographic location
—— Opportunities for family
—— Health
—— Growth potential
—— "Status" of church or pulpit
—— Amount of staff
—— Size of giving to missions
—— Nature of current program
—— Life style of the membership
—— Theological/political/social stance of congregation
—— Music
—— None of the above.

The purpose has been to help sort out some of the things which are important to you and why. Does it help any in setting priorities? Can you now realistically go back to your first three lists of ten and arrange them in order of importance to *you*?

In that classic, *The Will of God*, Leslie Weatherhead says there are two challenges to seeking God's will: (1.) Do we really want to know or are we trying to get his sanction for our own intentions? (2.) Do we have the courage to do God's will when we discern it? I am less ready to raise these questions, for it is my conviction that the restlessness of our middle years is a response to our desire to put our lives more deeply into God's hands and our ministry more completely in accord with the movement of his spirit in our world.

Check Points

There is a vagueness about our profession—vagueness inherent in ministering to the problems of people and the ills of society. Life and death, guilt and forgiveness, justice, mercy and love are all intangibles. The mystery of human existence doesn't come in measurable units. Meaning is not distributed in equal parts. Purpose cannot be determined by a compass. So it is difficult to know how we are doing.

This vagueness compounds itself when caught in the routine of twenty years of parish life. Even though a minister is surrounded by a variety of persons and involvements, each week has a sameness about it. The very competence which comes from experience can bring that "It-seems-that-I-have-been-through-this-before" feeling. Aware of the passing of time, or even of time running out, makes the mundane more miserable and the routine less romantic.

Dr. Carl A. Hammerschlag, psychiatrist-sculptor, has expressed his feelings of the "dis-ease" of middle-age. In a work called "Mid-Life Crisis" humankind is portrayed as being caught in a huge spider web. Circled with barbed wire, the web holds persons enmeshed and struggling yet unable to be free and ultimately the prey of the spider, death. All thrashing is in vain. All movement is limited. There is no evident purpose or hope. Many

can identify with this way of depicting the futile feelings of the middle years.

Being immobilized is no fun. Being caught in a web of circumstances saps our strength and soon we acquiesce. A sense of movement is integral to one's understanding of purpose. Routine has always been the enemy of fulfillment. Aimlessness, wandering, drifting may show lack of constraint but cannot be equated with freedom. They imply lack of direction, purpose and meaning. But they also suggest the absence of accomplishment or movement. They are static rather than active words. And they are dull.

Movement or activity are not ends in themselves. Busyness is part of our problem. Again and again we are baffled by how much we do and by how little we accomplish. No pastor at mid-career still believes that ''When the church is humming, the kingdom is coming.'' We have seen through that.

Being forty-nine and holding puts us in the same category with the sign post on a busy corner: Pointing directions but making no progress; aware of a destination but having no destiny. Purpose and progress, direction and distance, meaning and motion all go together. One way to break the routine is to divide time and tasks into manageable units. As each piece is completed there is a sense of accomplishment. Ultimately this can give us a positive attitude toward what we are doing, even routinely.

The purpose of this chapter is to suggest that one way out of the maze or web, if you prefer, is to set a course (goal) and to mark off the check points (objectives) which move us step by step until we are carried by our own momentum.

CHECK POINTS

Speaking as an old navigator, check points can keep us from being lost. These are identifiable points of reference on our route to the destination. They don't have the ultimate importance of goals. Yet, they are indicative of the direction and ground speed with which we are moving. Watching them disappear behind gives that sense of movement which reassures purpose and reaffirms destination. Comparing where we are to where we want to be allows for some mid-course corrections.

Management by objectives is big in industry and business. Variations on the theme of planning have captured the interests and energies of institutions. (Mager) Even the church rethinks its reason for being and organizes its resources to accomplish the ''great ends of the church.'' To call for the establishment of ''check points'' is not intended to give the full dignity of a planning process. But if one is to use time rather than just watch it slip by, if one is to set one's own agenda rather than be pressured into doing what others want, if one is to have a sense of purpose

I like a man, Cal, that chooses his goal early in life and never ceases backing up toward that end!

rather than frustration and discouragement, he must have those points of reference which confirm to his satisfaction that he is moving toward an end that *he* has chosen. Emerson has said, "At times the whole world seems to be in conspiracy to importune (us) with emphatic trifles." We must importune it with our own values.

This all came as quite a revelation to me the first time the Personnel Committee asked for my goals and objectives for the coming year. Getting them down on paper took some thought and experimenting. It also called for some sorting and choices. That first year was amateurish and, I confess, done with less enthusiasm than might be desirable. A combination of following directions and some trial and error finally resulted in some wording that was acceptable. They emphasized that the objectives should be measurable. The results, however, were great. I had a clearer sense of direction. It was possible to mark some progress. At the end of the year's activities, I could compare with the committee what had been planned and what had been accomplished. It was a reinforcing experience.

PSYCHOCARROTRY OR PSEUDOSTICKERY

The carrot and the stick are being challenged as adequate motivators in business and industry. They are anachronisms to the ministry. But if the clergy are not prompted by reward nor deterred by fear of punishment, what does get them moving?

It is my observation that most ministers desire to be responsible adults, willing and capable of looking after themselves; they find a satisfaction in work and achievement and want to make a contribution to society. There are few among us who are lazy. Our motivation does not come from supervision. It springs from commitment and conscience. We are the guardians of our standards, the authors of our objectives and, under God, the judges of our performance. We are most productive and satisfied when we are convinced that what we are doing is right and consistent with our understanding of God's will for our lives.

However, it helps to have these items stated as more than vague goals. Care must be taken to word these intentions or desires in such a manner that they can be understood by ourselves and others. They need to be clear enough that we know that we have reached the check point or where we are in relationship to it.

The greatest value in our writing objectives is that it makes it possible for us to evaluate our performance in more than a subjective way. A side effect is that it defuses the routine and gives a sense of movement.

Up until now a minister's work has been largely evaluated by either one of two ways: the highly subjective "I liked that sermon" or the highly objective method of counting the attendance. At least part of job satisfaction, however, is a sense of accomplishment. It is easier to know that a job has been done if it clear what the job is.

This would be adequate reason for taking time to state one's goals and objectives. Don't stop there, however. Be sure that these are shared with the official board. Not much has been done to assist sessions, trustees or vestries with "performance review" for clergy.

Assisting them in understanding your check points will give the basis for job evaluation and an arena in which to clarify expectations. Sharing with them in mutually accepted work objectives is

It just seems like where I've been and where I'm going are
the same place!

a real source of support. There is then a criteria by which to know
"how you are doing." It is the basis for your own personal judgment against what you know to be common understandings. To
be able to measure one's own progress is a much stronger motivation than carrots and sticks or rewards and punishments.

PUTTING IT ON PAPER

An objective is the opposite of the vagueness which opened
this chapter. First of all, it must be something which is *specific*.
General goals are great but they are difficult to pin down. State-

By the time I made out a complete list of all the things I needed to do today, it was too late to *do* them!

ments like "to be a better pastor" or "work for social justice" help point a direction but they are what Mager calls "Fussies." They are so big that it is not really possible to encompass all of their implications. By breaking these broad goals into some component parts, one can find some handles. What are some of the aspects of being a good pastor? One might list (a) calling on the shut-ins, (b) counseling with couples who plan to be married, (c) helping young people choose a life career. These are at least part of what is involved. They are identifiable and specific.

Or what are some of the ways to work for social justice? Here one could list such things as (a) promoting voter registration, (b) advocating for the unemployed, (c) demonstrating a concern for equal justice in the courts. These, too, are at least part of what is involved and they are specific.

Next, an objective must be *measurable.* Take the specific and tell how you will know that it has been accomplished. Following through on the desire to be a "good pastor," make (a) my objective will be to call on five shut-ins. By using one hand, it will be possible to know this objective has been reached. (b) My objective is to have two hours counseling with each couple before the wedding. (c) My objective is to expose the 25% of the youth in the congregation to three vocations.

Or to follow through on the intent of working for social justice. (a) My objective is to enroll 25 unregistered voters. (b) My objective is to find three audiences where Indian people can express

You're all doing exceptionally well with faith and hope, but
your charity was down about four per cent from last month!

their concern about the arrest ratio of Indians to non-Indians. (c)
My objective is to enlist ten people to monitor the superior court
system for one month.

The next criteria for an objective is that it be set in a time
frame. By when is it expected that the objective will have been
fulfilled? This may be the key to the sense of movement. Put a
deadline on the objective. *By the end of the week,* I will call on
five shut-ins. *Within the next two months,* I will have enrolled 25
unregistered voters. This time frame needs to be tailored to the
objective but be short enough to provide some motivation. Not
everyone works best under pressure applied externally. But some
of us can use a little self-imposed prodding—if the goal is something we value.

The time frame also provides a time for review. Our objective
provides the check points which mark movement or accomplish-

ment. Stagnation of spirit and discouragement often come from the feeling of futility—"spinning one's wheels." Being able to check off the objective or write "done" across the item brings its own reward. It is a time to celebrate!

But objectives also need to be *realistic*. They should not be too demanding. They should provide some push but should not smother. If the objective was to call upon five shut-ins this year, it would have hardly served much purpose. If the time frame was for this afternoon, it might have been impossible. Don't set goals which are beyond time, energy or dollar resources.

Objectives should also be *flexible*. They are to free us from routine. They are not another form of captivity. There will be times, many times, when objectives will need to be junked in order to respond to a mood, an opportunity, a crisis. Keep this sense of openness.

At the end of the time allowed, we ought to evaluate how realistic the objective was and make adjustments in our planning. This will be most productive if it is done regularly such as in connection with an annual job review.

If we don't, any attempt to use goals and objectives to give life some meaning or movement will be a bust. They should not add to discouragement. They should be a boost not a plague.

An objective should also be *personal*. Trying to measure ourselves by someone else's standard brings its own kind of reward. It may not be even closely related to what we want or need. Paul says, "Each one should judge his own conduct for himself . . . without having to compare it with what someone else has done."

Objectives then, should be specific, measurable, short-ranged, flexible, realistic and personal. Processes grow out of purpose. Setting goals and objectives is not some simple way of discovering the meaning of life, the significance of one's vocation or ultimate reality. It will not resolve our personal inconsistencies nor make us self-actualizing persons. But it will help us to make choices, to find accomplishment and if we share them with others, a basis for common expectations of what we are doing with our lives.

It Is Never Too Early

You, men and women in your forties and fifties who read this book. . . . Your life absorbs you to such an extent that you live it as if it must last forever. You know well that that is not the case. . . .

"Your manner of life now is already determining your life in those years of old age and retirement. Without realizing it even, and perhaps without your giving enough thought to it. One must therefore prepare oneself for retirement. . . ." (Tournier, *Learn to Grow Old*)

Retirement shocks many. Ministers are not exempt. One denomination is known to startle participants of their pension plan. On the member's fifty-fifth birthday comes a letter warning that the fateful day is only ten years away. There is always some uneasy joking at the office on that date! If you are 49 and holding, you will awake all too soon to read that little epistle.

The letter, of course, is a service. Ten years of planning for retirement will make it easier and more productive. So, fifteen years will be even better. And if experts are right, we should have been involved in retirement planning for many years.

Social Security payments, insurance premiums and contributions to a pension plan keep the idea of retirement in our consciousness. It might even make us think that we have been planning. Daydreaming about it can also be a substitute for plan-

Never view your retirement as the end of your useful years,
Cal, but rather as a new beginning of your declining ones!

ning. When one is in the muddle in the middle, this can also be an
escape from present frustrations. Fantasies about "early retirement" dance like sugar-plums through the mind of one seeking
some way out of an unhappy situation.

Planning for retirement is important. It gives perspective to the
middle-years. The possibilities of new life styles, the promise of
some leisure time, the prospects of an accumulation of a series of
postponed pleasures are intriguing. These we savor.

But retirement also holds the specter of ill health, of loss of
income and change in status. The fear of being a burden haunts
one's thinking. Loneliness and death cast their shadow on
thoughts of later years. Stephen Leacock wrote:

> Have you ever been out for a late afternoon walk, in the
> closing part of the afternoon, and suddenly looked up to
> realize that the leaves have practically all gone? And the sun
> has set and the day gone before you knew it—and with that

a cold wind blows across the landscape? That's retirement. . . . Have nothing to do with it. (Jones)

The four horsemen of the Apocalypse are best known to the
aged. Ministers have witnessed this and may have ambivalent
feelings about it. They may look forward with expectation or
want to "have nothing to do with it."

It seems that no one wants to die but neither does anyone want
to grow old. But to live is to grow old. The question is how to do it
graciously, creatively and meaningfully. How do I become a nice
old person?

PLAN AHEAD

There is a growing interest in planning for retirement.

Good lord, Gladys, a few short years from now, these will be the good old days!

Shouldn't there be preparation for this stage of life as for one's younger years? The adjustments may actually be more traumatic because so many things can happen within such a relatively short period of time. I once talked with widows of two ministers whose husbands both retired, moved to a new part of the country and died—all within eighteen months. In our more youthful years, we did not face as many shocks as these two did in that eighteen-month period.

An announcement of "The First Annual National Conference on Pre-Retirement" just came to my office. Some of the subjects to be included on the agenda were: "Pre-Retirement Planning: Social Responsibility, Self-Interest or Both?"; "The Changing World of Work and Its Ramifications for Pre-Retirement Planning"; "Future Trends in Pre-Retirement Planning."

The psychiatrist team of Jonas and Jonas believe, "The single most important thing a person in the middle years can do to insure a satisfactory old age is to get his mind 'tuned in' and, so far as

I'm a retired minister! Some of us *know* when to quit!

possible accustomed in advance to any changes that will have to be made, so that he can prepare for them." (Jonas)

All of this just documents our need to plan ahead. Fortunately, most ministers have some control over the exact time of their retirement and therefore should be more prepared.

Here are some of the areas in which changes can be expected:

TIME ON MY HANDS

Although most of my retired friends complain that they are busier than ever, the reallocation of time is the most obvious adjustment one makes when retiring. ''Leisure time'' may not fit our concept of retirement but there are certainly some new freedoms in how one uses time—unless one doesn't know how to use time. In that case, there will be either a frenzied rush to fill all hours since being busy is the only measure of a person's worth. Or there will be frustration and disillusionment. How one handles his or her time will affect health, self-esteem, spouse relationships and finances. Three retirees whose lives have been spent in assisting others face personal adjustment agree that one must begin to develop a ''second occupation'' in middle years if one is to make the time adjustment at retirement. This post retirement career need not be a professional position but it must be something that is satisfying. It must demand respect in the person's mind requiring a skill and growth in achievement. Puttering in the garden will soon become a chore. Learning to cross-breed tomatoes or graft fruit trees may give recognition as well as pleasure. The socializing may make fun out of stuffing envelopes for United Way but it won't be as fulfilling as being chairman of one section of the campaign. Travel to strange places fills several weeks with fascination but doing enough research to be able to write or lecture on those places with authority will bring months or years of returns.

More and more attention has been turned to the reservoir of skill and experience presented by people in retirement. It is difficult to place a dollar value on this but it is certainly in the billions. More important, the impact on these individuals in terms of frustration, despair and loss of dignity is beyond computation.

Our first problem, then, will be to adjust to our use of time. The adjustment starts now as we develop our attitude toward our job and present leisure time. This will be the key to how we use our ''enforced leisure.'' If we don't know what to do with ourselves when we aren't busy or in demand, we can anticipate some problems when we are out of sight and out of mind. Ministers in mid-career who have grown ''accustomed to the pace''—who have allowed other's demands to set the schedule especially need to take that day off each week. They need to be confronted by some

You know what worries me about retiring, Cal? I've spent so many years *looking* for ways to avoid work, I'm afraid I won't know what to do with my time when I don't have to *look* anymore!

free time and not be cowed and to find some meaningful "retirement occupation possibilities apart from the vocation of the ordained clergy." This will enhance the acceptance of the new role of senior citizen. The clergy have one big advantage, since their skills are those used in voluntary institutions there is good probability that there will be places within the church or community where they can continue to do "their thing." However, they may find it more challenging to tackle some new types of service.

YOU IN MY ARMS

Couples who have lived together through the middle years will have grown increasingly dependent upon each other. After the children have grown and gone, there will have been deepening times of togetherness. Retirement brings another period of adjustment in relationships. Being around the house will fill a much larger part of life than was formerly devoted to the job. Mutual considerations are essential. The house will seem smaller and for a while you may even get in each other's way. This time, however, can be agreeably helpful and if both husband and wife are thoughtful, there will be many opportunities to express understanding and appreciation.

But what happens when death strikes? One psychologist says flatly, "The loss of a spouse is the principal trauma of old-age." How can one prepare for this shock? How does one deal with loneliness? Henri Nouwen doesn't give a direct answer to these questions but suggests that part of being human is this yearning sense of loneliness. It haunts us at all ages of life. It can never really be satisfied through any personal relationships, however meaningful, nor through any groups, however supportive. Part of our very ministry has been to share these feelings with those we have served. "This is a very hard call, because for a minister who is committed to forming a community of faith, loneliness is a very painful wound which is easily subject to denial and neglect. But once the pain is accepted and understood, a denial is no longer necessary, and ministry can be a healing service." (Nouwen)

In the aftermath of death, the sorrow will still be acutely real. Hurt will bleed into tears. But for one who has resolved estrangement, who has worked through disappointment and dealt with failure in trying to create the perfect community, there is not only power to face death, there is power to minister to life.

The deeper the love, the sharper is the pain. This is not counsel for either superficial relationships or shallow commitments. Even when two have been truly one, there can never be complete dependence for even these ties will be broken. All ties but those to Christ are passing.

When one has dealt with one's own personal security and how to handle all this "spare" time, there are still some questions which one ought to stake out as he looks forward to retirement.

WHERE ARE YOU GOING TO LIVE—In what house, that is?

If you have lived in a manse or parsonage, you have been at a disadvantage. You have no equity in a house. This might be a

Isn't that cute? He thinks you're hurting me!

good time to ask your congregation to sell the manse and give you
a housing allowance so that you can purchase your own home.
With careful management over a fifteen-year period, you should
build up some equity. The amount will vary from city to city and
from year to year. During the last ten years in my area, the price
of real estate has increased on the average of about 6% per year.
Since a minister does not report the housing allowance as income

and can include both interest and taxes on his deductions, he has an added advantage in building an equity. The value of the house owned by your congregation is really part of your salary. Had it been paid in cash, it would have accrued to your benefit.

Not all is glamour, however. Hot water heaters go out at the most inopportune times. Taxes never cease and come in big chunks. Insurance, painting, roofing all become your responsibilities. Owning a house can be a drag if you want to move. Without allowing for appreciation, it takes about five years of monthly payments to build up an equity equal to a real estate broker's commission.

WHERE ARE YOU GOING TO LIVE—Area, that is?

There are some merits to deciding early where to live after retirement. One persistent question: Do we stay in the last parish? We feel at home and are hopefully among friends. But how would we have felt to have the former pastor as a member of our parish? Better still, how will our successor feel to have *us* around?

If we decide not to stay, there are a whole series of questions: Do we move to a new area where maybe the weather is mild? How about a retirement community like Sun City or a retirement complex like Plaza Del Monte? Do we want to serve a small congregation unable to afford a pastor or on the staff of a larger church on a part-time basis? Do we want to be close to our family? Is proximity to cultural enrichment possibilities important?

Obviously, personal preferences will play a major role in resolving these questions. By starting now, it is possible to experiment with answers and to explore alternatives. Use your vacations to search out the kind of dream retirement that you both agree is wanted. I have been living in an area attractive to retirees. Some come and are enthusiastic. Others are unable to make the transition and return "home" sadder but wiser.

In planning ahead for retirement, both in location and in style of housing, it is important to do so with the death of one member of the marriage weighed as a possibility. Approximately one-half of all retirees are still living as couples. The other fifty percent will be a survivor, with widows out-numbering widowers. Would you make the same plans for retirement for one as you plan for two? That time will come.

GETTING THE LEGAL MATTERS IN ORDER

Long before a will is needed, it must be prepared. Who knows when it will be needed? If you haven't made a will, do it now. Since a will does not become effective until death, the making of one does not restrict the right to revoke or alter its terms unless such action would violate contractural obligations then existing.

Many ministers procrastinate assuming that their estate is not worth the effort. Don't be modest. Even without extensive holdings, when one adds an equity in house, savings, insurance benefits and accrued pensions, the total might impress you. If you don't decide what will happen to your possessions, the court will and your family may not like the results.

There seems to be much confusion about the costs of asset transfer at the time of a person's death. An attorney friend, Tom Wade, puts it this way: "Regardless of the size of your estate, it is strongly recommended that you discuss with an attorney its components and your desires for their ultimate disposition. Such forethought may result in substantial savings in inheritance taxes, administration expenses and delay in settling the estate.

"If you reside in one of the eight community property states (Arizona, California, Idaho, Louisiana, Nevada, New Mexico, Texas and Washington) the laws regulating property ownership and descent require special consideration.

"Inheritance taxes are separately imposed by the Federal Government and states, and are determined by the size of the estate. Contrary to widely held belief, joint ownership by a husband and wife does not relieve their holdings from such taxes, except to the extent that the surviving spouse establishes his or her contribu-

It says my uncle Clifford passed away and mentioned me in his will! He didn't leave me anything, he just mentioned me!

tion to the original cost. Under the Federal law an estate is entitled to a $60,000.00 exemption. State exemptions vary. For non-community property states, the Federal Estate Tax Law, in addition to the $60,000.00 exemption, allows a deduction of up to fifty percent of the total value of the estate, less taxes, administration expenses, debts and certain losses for property of a descendant left to his or her spouse. Technical requirements for assuring the benefit of this deduction makes professional guidance imperative and should be sought from your bank or attorney.''

As you have your will drawn, give thought to including your church as a beneficiary. This is stewardship of accumulated resources. It is as important as stewardship of income although it does not receive as much attention. Including your church or favorite mission project will be one way of continuing support to that for which you have given your life. Most denominations have persons who can help you with wording and by providing continuing management of funds you might leave.

There will be times in retirement when the services of a law firm or the counsel of an attorney will be needed. It will be most reassuring if you have already selected your ''friendly attorney.''

Your needs will not be restricted to wills. Buying or selling a home, guidance in purchase of certain securities, advice in estate planning are all easier if you have confidence in your attorney. Hopefully he should know you and how you think. Establishing and building a relationship now will give a sense of reliability that will be appreciated when the need arises.

TAKE NO THOUGHT FOR THE MORROW

How does a Christian minister make plans for retirement? Doesn't Jesus say "take no thought for tomorrow, what you shall eat and what you shall drink . . ." He also told a parable of the wise and foolish virgins and oddly enough, the wise ones had planned ahead. There is no doubt about our ability to get so tied up in possessions or so convinced we can take care of ourselves that we don't seek first the Kingdom of God. This is a fact of life we have known all of our ministry. But also give some thought to your stewardship of the resources which have been entrusted to you. This will involve doing some thinking about money. You'd better do some of that thinking now because it will affect how you face the future when you retire. Concerns over financial matters are an overwhelming preoccupation of retired persons. Fear that the reserves are not adequate to meet a major medical problem, indecisiveness about investments, fretting over the payment of bills all plague the days of the retiree. No planning can guarantee peace of mind but it can alleviate some of the booby traps. Here are some hints:

——Find someone with financial skills to assist you in estate planning. Professional help may be too expensive unless you have a sizable portfolio. However, there must be a person in your congregation or in a neighboring parish who will give some help. Choose experienced and wise counsel but don't abdicate your own responsibilities to judgment. Get a balanced view. Anyone selling insurance will probably be oriented toward insurance as a method of saving. A stockbroker will tend to recommend stocks. One who sells mutual funds most likely believes in their future

and a good banker will have confidence in his company's certificates of deposit. Each has its merits and each has its limitations.
——Both husband and wife should be involved in the decisions about money matters. We are talking about the future. No one knows who will be around the longest. Our society is full of widows who suddenly find themselves confronted by income tax forms, paid and unpaid bills and a stack of decisions about how to invest the proceeds of a life insurance policy when for 40 years they never were even asked to balance the checkbook.
——Review the provision of insurance policies and pension plans. Most give options as to how the benefits are to be paid. There can be electives between the amounts paid to a couple or a division which will provide a larger share to a surviving spouse. The reason for choices is that no one plan meets all needs. Which will best serve you?
——So much is written about the need for a savings program to supplement pension and social security that I won't add to the words on this subject. It is good advice. Some regular, monthly plan is about the only one that really works.
——Explore the benefits of a tax-sheltered annuity plan. With the children no longer a tax deduction, there may be double value in this as a savings program.
——Develop and keep a file of up-dated information on the whereabouts of important papers: wills, insurance policies, securities, bank accounts, safe boxes. A bank will need to impound a safe box until an inventory can be made. It is wise, therefore, to keep some duplicate copies of information at home. Your attorney will have a copy of your will. Let's hope that it has been revised periodically.
——An annual financial status report can be helpful in tracing one's progress toward retirement goals. This is sometimes called a statement of net worth. A form for this can be obtained from your bank. It is also useful in checking to see that one's resources are going where they are intended.
——If you do not have any training or experience in money management, this would be a practical area for some learning

What it boils down to is, our early retirement fund has retired earlier than *we* have!

experiences. In retirement, making ends meet can be the name of the game. Satisfaction can come from knowing that you are getting the most out of your dollars. That no one is taking advantage of you will be its own reward.

One survey in Canada indicated that pre-retirement strain and worry can cause up to a 20% loss in productivity. This may be high for clergy but there is enough truth to prompt us to plan ahead. Drake University which has had the wisdom to establish a Pre-Retirement Planning Center proclaims, "There comes a point in time when a summation of achievements culminates, then begins anew . . . refreshed, more powerful and more experienced than before. This is the new horizon of the retired person."

According to my figures we could retire next month on a fixed annual income of twenty six dollars, and forty eight cents!

PREPARING A SPOUSE SURVIVAL KIT

Often only the "record keeper" in the family knows the whereabouts of important papers. A decapacitating illness or death can cause havoc in the financial affairs of a family. An insurance premium missed, a bond maturing or a missed mortgage payment might cause either embarrassment or financial loss to the family. The following pages list information which should be immediately available. Since it needs to be up-dated periodically, it is suggested that the forms be copied on letter-size paper and duplicated. Adapt it to your needs by adding or subtracting lines. On January 1, of each year, check to see if there needs to be any changes made in the records.

. . . if I should die before I wake, please look after my
philodendrons!

AN INDEX OF IMPORTANT PAPERS AND/OR INFORMATION

When reference is made to a Safety Deposit Bank, it refers to
Box# _____ in _____ (Branch) of the _____
_____ Bank. The key is located _____
_____
_____, _____, _____
_____ are the signers on record with the bank.
   When reference is made to a file or drawer in the home it refers
to _____
_____
_____ (describe).

PAPERS/INFORMATION	LOCATION	COMMENT
Wills: Husband		Our Attorney's name and address:
Wife		
Marriage License		

Birth Certificates:
      Husband
      Wife
      Children (list)

Social Security Card
and Number:
      Husband
      Wife

Military Discharge:
      Husband
      Wife
Deeds:
      Residence   Insured with

            (others)
                                       (agent's name)

Title of Ownership:
      Car   Name of Insurance
                                         Agent

      Car
      Boat, etc.

Life Insurance Policies

                                         Agent's Name

Stocks and Bonds   Give Broker's
                                       Name

Savings Books or
   Certificates of
   Deposit

We have the following
  Bank Accounts:

      Checking Acct.

                            branch   bank

      Checking Acct.

                            branch   bank

      Savings Acct.

                            branch   bank

                            branch   bank

    Other:

PERSONAL FINANCIAL STATEMENT 19_

ASSETS	LIABILITIES
CASH	PAYABLES (Schedule X)
Checking	
Checking	MORTGAGES (See Schedule A)
Savings (or C.O.)	
	LOANS PAYABLE ON INSURANCE
	(Schedule C)
	OTHER LIABILITIES
RECEIVABLES	
STOCKS & BONDS (Schedule B)	
CASH VALUE OF INSURANCE	
(Schedule C)	

TAXES PAYABLE

TOTAL ASSETS
TOTAL LIABILITIES
NET WORTH

The following schedules are merely guidelines—individual needs may warrant the use of additional space.

S C H E D U L E A—Real Estate   Deed Location:

Location	Purchase Costs (w/improvements)	Estimated Value	Amount Owing	Net Value

S C H E D U L E B—Stocks, Bonds and Mutual Funds   Securities Location:

Security	Number Shares	Book Value	Market Value 1/1/74	Market Value 12/31/74	Change + or −	1974 Dividends	% Yield
Totals							

S C H E D U L E C—Life Insurance   Policy Location:

Company	Amount	Cash Value 1/1/74	Cash Value 12/31/74	Increase	Loans
Totals					

S C H E D U L E D—Health & Accident Insurance   Policy Location:

Company	Amount	Comment

S C H E D U L E E—Casualty/Automobile   Policy Location:

Policy	Company	Items Covered

S C H E D U L E F—Pension/Social Security Credits

	Credits 12/31/73	Credits 12/31/74	Projected Income at 65
Social Security			

S C H E D U L E X—Payables (other than mortgages—see Schedule A)

Payable To	Purpose	Amount Due 12/31/73	Amount Due 12/31/74	Change + or −
Totals				

We Can Do It

What does one minister say to another pilgrim through the depressions, the haunting questions, the weariness, the loneliness of middle-age? "We can do it!" Not by will nor by might but by the grace and power of God in Christ.

In those years immediately after World War II, it took a pretty poor preacher to keep people away from church. Expectations of peace stimulated thoughtful persons to seek a "more excellent way." Young parents sought the church for themselves and for their children. Many of us went through the worries and the excitement of a building program. All watched the charts go up and up. Three services on a Sunday morning were not uncommon. Membership climbed. Giving doubled and tripled.

But the bloom faded. There was a challenge to the comfortable pew by provocative theologians. We awoke to learn that God was dead. The disinherited of the earth were making claims for retribution and a place on the councils of the church and society. Our children turned their backs on all that we thought so important and they wanted to do their "thing" and do it now. Institutions which had long been held in high esteem were called the "enemies of the people." Our nation was torn apart with a controversial war. New words like "Watergate" and "plumbers" began to define human frailty in government. Church attendance dropped.

Now that I have your attention!

Church bureaucracies were shaken and challenged and disempowered.

And to top it all this middle-age disease!

Is it any wonder that we are discouraged and restless?

But, my friend, this is the kind of time which refines our basic commitments. Our maturity and our experience have pushed us up against the roots of our faith. One cannot be immersed in the daily round of a pastor's life without being confounded by both the hurts and the hopes of human existence. The questions which have been bugging us through our middle years are of the essence of life. Observed in others, they have come back to catch us off guard.

If it's all the same to you, Les, I'd just as soon shake your hand as grapple for it!

But we can do it! Forced to the source of our ultimate strength, we find more than survival. New assurance comes. We *do* know who we are. We *do* know what is important. We *do* want to conserve those things for which we have been investing our lives.

No one needs to remind us of our weaknesses. These were apparent to us when we made our first response to God. We should not be surprised by the frailty and sin of our society or of ourselves. This we have witnessed for more than twenty-five years. Failure should not sap our strength for there is forgiveness and acceptance and love.

Howard Thurman reminds us, "There is no harder lesson to learn in the spiritual life than the fact that results belong to God. A man's responsibility is to seek before God how to purge his life of those things that make for error and wrong choices, and to act in the light of his best wisdom and most profound integrity. Beyond this, the results are in God's hands. Of course, a man is never free of the sense of responsibility for results, but this is ultimately a gratuitous concern on his part." (Thurman)

For a minister, it may well be that success is really more difficult to handle than failure. Paul reminds us that we have this treasure of faith in clay pots so that we will not confuse our doings with the real source of our power. When things go well, it is easy to lay claim to the laurels—in Jack Horner fashion, to say, "what a big boy (or girl) am I." When God is not acknowledged in our successes, there is no one who stands by us in our failures.

The church has been closest to greatness in the times of trial and testing. When it has been rich, it has grown soft and vain. When it has been influential, it has confused this with righteousness. When it has held power, it has thought that it was God.

And, haven't we, too, been the least aware of God's presence when all seemed to be going well?

It might be that this crisis in the mid-point of our career is the way that God sends us back to the basics, forces us to reexamine those things in which we have really come to trust and to question those things which society has called values. As Augustine said, our spirits are restless until they find their rest in God.

A couple of years ago, my job as Synod Executive of Arizona was to be terminated with the formation of the new Synod of the Southwest. The date was set. My future was unknown. My dossier was in a stack of those being considered for the position of Executive in the new synod. There was a long period of uncertainty. At that point, I was forty-eight and drifting. I was concerned for my family's welfare. There was a sense of commitment to assisting with the orderly transition to the new organization. Friends and family were helpful, listening patiently to hours of self-evaluation and searching. Feeling that the Com-

. . . and please grant me humility . . . with just a smattering of class!

mittee could not resolve the tension which might exist between the two previous synods, I weighed removing my name from further consideration. Then one day it came into focus. I was reading *Survival Plus* by Reuel Howe. He talked about the person who has within himself the capacity to deal with strange and challenging situations and I knew that with God's help I could be that kind of a person. He wrote of a friend who "is sufficiently secure to know that no matter what happened to him and those with whom he is associated, he will be able to respond to it in some constructive way. He is secure enough to include himself in any situation and any situation in himself. He has developed creative powers of survival.''

My faith in God's purposes and my awareness of his quiet leading in the past were all there to reassure me. I knew that it might involve moving, learning some new skills and boning up on some forgotten ones. The possibilities of less salary, less freedom and less status were all put in perspective. I knew then and I know now God can and will use me in any kind of a future that evolves if I will let him.

We put our house up for sale. The question of whether to leave my name in for consideration no longer plagued my thoughts. A new sense of freedom welcomed the future. A new sense of confidence greeted uncertain tasks. I was confident and calm. By accepting life and myself but most of all by the awareness of God's presence, I was getting it all together.

It is strange that in middle-age, when we are at our peak, the future should intimidate us. Seasoned and experienced, we become conservative, reverting to what has worked before, we limit our potential. We ought to be confident to try new things. To use our experience as a base from which to venture instead of a place to hide. To use our accumulated ''know-how'' as the well trained professional rather than a comfortable habit.

My friend, it has not yet occurred to us what we might become. This is not a time to stop dreaming or venturing. ''Sometimes dreams are the cry of the heart for the boundless and unexplored, the untried, the unknown.'' That restlessness within is a prompting to grow in spirit, in commitment, in usefulness.

This can well begin by living as more open persons, welcoming new adventures and exploring new relationships. One summer I spent a week on a high country trail ride. In the magnificence of a wilderness area, thirty of us rode trails through spruce and aspen. Above the timberline, we literally looked down on rainbows. As overwhelming as the scenery was, the great thing for me was to be treated as a person. I was ''Dick'' the character riding ''Brown Jug.'' Gone were the titles and bad jokes about the ''bishop.''

I used to dread tomorrow, reverend . . . now I dread all of next year!!

Minister, doctor, teacher, cowhand, we were all just people on the trail, around the campfire or doing chores.

If we could only realize that we don't need to prove ourselves. How many times do we need to be reminded, neither to God nor man.

It was God who loved us into life even before we knew him.

It was God who called us to a ministry.

It was God who guided us even when we were unaware.

It was God who brooded over our ministry with expectancy.

How dare we forget!

I was forty-nine when I started this book: forty-nine and holding—back. Still uncertain about myself, apprehensive about the future.

Now I am fifty-one. All the tension has not vanished. Neither the world nor I have changed all that much but I'm beginning ever

so easily, ever so surely to let go. There is no packaged optimism, no forced smile. But there is a deeper faith and a real basis for hope.

At the time of writing there are announcements for a new book. The publicity says it is for "Adventurers." Those who are willing to "take the plunge." I intend to read it for this is what I sense life to be—an adventure. There will be risk and exposure, new obstacles to manage, long stretches of desert to cross. But there will also be new friends, fresh scenery, tasks to accomplish, un-marred opportunity.

The adventure does not stop at mid-career. It is from this van-

I'm convinced, Cal . . . yours is a case of overindulging in moderation!

tage point that we can look back, get our bearings, and make some mid-point corrections.

We will continue to have the desire to return to "our own turf" where we feel secure among trusted friends and familiar fare. But we can't go back or stand still for our security must come from another source and other relationships.

To accept and to relish what is past gives depth and color to the present. To cling to it or be obsessed with it impoverishes our present and steals our future. It is natural to feel disappointment over failures or some guilt about past mistakes. But we need to accept our limitations, our humanness and move on. There is much ahead that needs our attention.

During this time, I have also gained new perspectives on the church. I am hopeful for its future not because it has been reorganized although that may make it more efficient. Not because there is a new participation by laymen in the decision-making processes although this is encouraging. Not because it has become more sensitive to the wounds of the world although this is of its essence. Not because God loves it. I know well, that he loves the world and not just the church. But there is evidence that the church is loved with the love of a father who has nurtured it and who has dreams for it.

I have hope for the church because it is the very God who has reached into our lives to make them whole, who has pulled together our fractured and broken spirits and given meaning and purpose. It is he who called us in earlier years, who calls us now and who is our promise for the future.

> *To dream the impossible dream,*
> *To fight the unbeatable foe,*
> *To bear with unbearable sorrow,*
> *To run where the brave dare not go . . .*
> *To run where the brave dare not go,*
> *Though the goal be forever too far,*
> *To try, though you are* way worn *and* weary,
> *To reach the unreachable star. . . . . ***

Be patient with us, Lord, we're coming!

* The Impossible Dream, song, from the musical play, *Man of La Mancha*, lyrics by Joe Darion and music by Mitch Leigh. © MCMLXV Andrew Scott, Inc., Helena Music Corp., Sam Fox Publishing Co. Inc. Sam Fox Publishing Company, Inc., sole agent. All rights reserved. International copyright secured. Used by permission.

Bibliography

Ellis, H. F., *Mediatrics*. William Morrow & Co., New York 1962.

Fried, Barbara, *The Middle-Age Crisis*. Harper & Row, Publishers, Inc., New York 1967.

Barrett, Myrtice J., *Review of Literature of Mid-Life Crisis For Males*. Unpublished paper, Arizona State University, College of Nursing, 1973.

Changing Careers—Five Americans Begin Again in their Middle-Years, Life Magazine, June 12, 1970.

Lee, Robert and Casebier, Marjorie, *The Spouse Gap: Weathering the Marriage Crisis During Middlescence*. Abingdon Press, Nashville and New York, 1971.

Schanche, Don A., *What Happens—Emotionally and Physically —When a Man Reaches 40*, Today's Health, March, 1973.

Saxes, L. P., *Sex and the Mature Man*. Gilbert Press, New York, 1969.

Pooped Generation, Changing Times, December, 1969.

Drucker, Peter F., *The Age of Discontinuity: Guidelines to Our Changing Society*. Harper & Row, Publishers, Inc., New York and Evanston, 1968-69.

Scarf, Maggie, *Husbands in Crisis*. McCalls, June, 1972.

Bolles, Richard Nelson, *What Color is Your Parachute*. Copyright 1970 by Richard Nelson Bolles, 627 Taylor Street, 22, San Francisco, California 94102.

Jud, Gerald J.; Burch, Genevieve Walters, and Mills, Edgar W.,

Jr., *Ex-Pastors: Why Men Leave the Parish Ministry.* Pilgrim Press, Philadelphia and Boston, 1970.

Smith, Donald, *Clergy in The Cross Fire.* Westminster Press. 1973.

Nouwen, Henri J. M., *The Wounded Healer: Ministry in Contemporary Society.* Doubleday & Co., Inc., Garden City, New York, 1972.

Erikson, Erik H., *Gandhi's Truth: On the Origins of Militant Nonviolence.* W. W. Norton & Co., Inc., New York, 1969.

Thurman, Howard, *The Mood of Christmas.* Harper & Row, Publishers, Inc., New York, 1973.

Tournier, Paul, *Learn to Grow Old.* Harper & Row, Publishers, Inc., New York, 1972.

Rilke, Rainer Maria, *Translations from the Poetry of Rainer Maria Rilke,* translated by M. V. Herton Norton, W. W. Norton & Co., New York, 1962. (The Norton Library)

Aulen, Gustaf, *Dag Hammerskjold's White Book.* Fortress Press, Philadelphia, 1969.

LeShan, Eda J., *The Wonderful Crisis of Middle Age.* David McKay Co., New York, 1973.

Rogers, Kenn, *The Mid-Career Crisis,* Saturday Review of the Society, January 1, 1973, p. 37-38.

Sueltz, Arthur F., *When the Wood is Green.* Harper & Row, Publishers, Inc., New York, 1973.

Bonhoeffer, Dietrich, *Letters and Papers from Prison.* Revised ed., The MacMillan Co., New York, 1953.

President's Council on Physical Fitness, *Adult Physical Fitness,* U. S. Government Printing Office, Washington, D.C.

Novak, Michael, *The Catholic Case for Contraception,* "Frequent, Even Daily Communion," edited by Daniel Cullahan, MacMillan & Co., London, 1969, p. 98.

Wyse, Lois, *Love Poems for the Very Married.* 5th Printing, The World Publishing Co., Cleveland and New York, 1968.

Hall, Mary Harrington, *A Conversation with Peter F. Drucker,* Psychology Today.

Tournier, Paul, *To Resist or to Surrender.* 4th Printing, John Knox Press, Richmond, Virginia, 1972.

Hadden, Jeffrey K., *Confusion and Hope: Clergy and Laity and the Church in Transition.* Edited by Glenn R. Bucher and Patricia R. Hill, Fortress Press, Philadelphia, 1974, p. 15-16.

Bach, George R., and Wyden, Peter, *The Intimate Enemy.* 5th ed., Avon Books, New York, 1971.

Drucker, Peter *Management, Tasks, Responsibilities, Practices.* Harper & Row, Publishers, Inc., New York, 1974.

Levinson, Daniel J., et al. "The Psychosocial Development of Men in Early Adulthood and the Mid-Life Transition," *Life History Research in Psychopathology*, edited by D. F. Ricks, A. Thomas and M. Roff, vol. 3, University of Minnesota Press, 1974.

Vocation Agency, The United Presbyterian Church, U.S.A., *Pastoral Development Inventory*, 1974.

Weatherhead, Leslie D., *The Will of God.* Abingdon Press, New York and Nashville, 1944.

Mager, Robert F., *Goal Analysis*, Fearon Publishers, Belmont, California, 1972.

Mager, Robert F., *Preparing Objectives For Programmed Instruction.* Fearon Publishers, San Francisco, California, 1962.

Jones, David, and Jones, Doris, *Young Till We Die.* Coward, McCann & Geoghegan, Inc., New York, 1973.

Thurman, Howard, *Disciplines of the Spirit.* Harper & Row, Publishers, New York, 1963.

Howe, Reuel L., *Survival Plus.* The Seabury Press, New York, 1971.

ADDITIONAL HELPFUL READING

Arthur, Julietta K., *Return to Action: A Guide to Voluntary Service.* Abingdon Press, Nashville and New York, 1969.

Better Health After Fifty, A Retirement Council Publication, New York, 1964.

Bowers, Margaretta K., M.D., *Conflicts of the Clergy.* Nelson, 1964.

Franzblau, Rose N., *The Middle Generation.* Holt, Rinehart & Winston, New York, 1971.

Howe, Reuel L., *The Changing Years*. The Seabury Press, New York, 1959.

Miller, Keith, *The Becomers*. Word Books, Publisher, Waco, Texas, 1973.

Neugarten, B., *Middle-age and Aging*. Chicago University Press, Chicago, 1968.

Material for the Educational Research Information Center related to this subject is available from ERIC Clearinghouse on Counseling and Personal Services, University of Michigan, School of Education Building Room 2108, Ann Arbor, Mich. 40814.